'A FAVOURITE STUDY'
BUILDING THE KING'S INNS

'A FAVOURITE STUDY'

BUILDING THE KING'S INNS

PATRICIA M^CCARTHY

GILL & MACMILLAN

Gill & Macmillan Ltd
Hume Avenue
Park West
Dublin 12
with associated companies throughout the world
www.gillmacmillan.ie

ISBN-13: 978 07171 4162 3
ISBN-10: 0 7171 4162 4
Print origination by Design Image, Dublin
Printed by Butler & Tanner, Frome, Somerset

The paper used in this book is made from the wood pulp of managed forests. For every tree felled, at least one tree is planted, thereby renewing natural resources.

A catalogue record is available for this book from the British Library.

1 3 5 4 2

CONTENTS

LIST OF ILLUSTRATIONS

FOREWORD

While the King's Inns has been formally in existence since 1541, its commissioned and surviving properties date from only 1800. Perhaps, however, we were fortunate in having had to wait almost three centuries as we were then in a position to retain the services of a number of the leading architectural practitioners for the execution, in particular, of our dining hall and the library building. Despite a constant shortage of funds, the society has always managed to erect or acquire buildings that continue to make a major contribution to the cityscape of Dublin, not least to 'Dublin's street of palaces', Henrietta Street.

As our requirements changed, a number of interventions to these properties were found to be necessary. Over time, however, some of our records had become blurred and we were not always clear as to the precise nature of the works carried out by the society's architects. With this in mind, we asked Patricia McCarthy to undertake a full survey of all our properties. Her research has yielded an amount of new material, not least of which is correspondence between the architect of the King's Inns, James Gandon, and the society's building committee during the period 1803 to 1805. To our delight and complete satisfaction, the benchers are now in a position to commend to you this scholarly study.

John L. Murray
Chief Justice
September 2006

ACKNOWLEDGMENTS

Writing this account of the buildings of the King's Inns has been at once a pleasure and a responsibility. The pleasure was researching in such beautiful and historic surroundings. The responsibility was treading in the footsteps of Edward McParland who is not only a biographer of the architect James Gandon, but someone who knows these historic buildings intimately, and who has shared his knowledge of them through his many publications. Without his scholarship to guide me, this work would have been much more difficult and would have been a lengthier process. I am deeply grateful for his advice and encouragement.

Most of my research was conducted in the archive of the King's Inns library in Henrietta Street. My sincerest thanks to Jonathan Armstrong, the society's librarian who, together with Isabel Duggan, David Curran and all of the staff in the King's Inns, could not have been more accommodating or patient with me: it was a pleasure to work among them.

I am grateful to Colum Kenny, whose writings on the history of the society I have plundered shamelessly. Particular thanks go to Anthony Malcomson for reading the text and for his many suggestions. My thanks also to Christine Casey, Michael and Aileen Casey, Cathal Crimmins, David Davison, the late Conor Griffin, David Griffin and the staff of the Irish Architectural Archive, Ian Lumley, Charles Lysaght, William Maguire, Jane Meredith and John Montague, all of whom have helped in many ways. Needless to say, all opinions and errors are solely my own.

The under-treasurer of the society, Camilla McAleese, has been the driving force behind the book. Her encouragement and enthusiasm were infectious and I am very grateful to her and to the benchers and Council of the King's Inns for the opportunity to write it.

Finally, thanks to my husband Fenton, and my children Simon, Ross and Kate, for their constant support and love.

BY THE LIFFEY: ESTABLISHING THE INNS

The earliest surviving printed map of Dublin, published by John Speed in 1610 as part of his study of Ireland and Britain, clearly indicates the site of the inns, on the north bank of the River Liffey, directly across from the walls of the city of Dublin and beside the city's only bridge. The site extended to about three acres and was the property of the 'Blackfriars', as the Dominican friary of St Saviour's had long been known (Fig. 1.1).[1]

The city of Dublin in 1610 was surrounded by walls punctured at intervals by gates. Almost rectangular in shape, it lay to the south of the River Liffey with one of its long sides bordering the river.[2] The most important buildings on Speed's map are Dublin Castle in the south-east corner, Christchurch Cathedral in the centre, St Patrick's Cathedral situated outside the walls to the south, and Queen Elizabeth's newly founded Trinity College to the east. Across Old Bridge, which spanned the Liffey, lay the parish of St Michan's in Oxmantown in which Blackfriars was located.

In 1539, during the Reformation, the friary had been surrendered to the Crown following the passing of an Act for the suppression of religious houses. Blackfriars would have been known to a number of legal practitioners in Dublin. In Trinity term 1520 its hall was used as a temporary location for sessions of the courts of justice, and each year on Michaelmas day a sermon on the duties of magistrates was preached in the friary church in the presence of the mayor and aldermen of Dublin. Seeing an opportunity to establish the first Irish inn of court on this riverside site, it appears that the lawyers took possession of the former friary as soon as it was vacated in July 1539.[3] There they 'kept commons' or gathered to dine, and called their new foundation 'the Kinges Inn', in honour of King Henry VIII.[4] In August 1541 the lawyers sought security of tenure of the site and petitioned the privy council in England for title to Blackfriars. A twenty-one-year lease was granted early in 1542 followed by another, four years after the expiration of the first, in 1567. But progress on the establishment of a thriving inn of court stalled and by the end of the sixteenth century the society had lost possession of most, if not all, of Blackfriars which was then being used as a military storehouse.[5]

As the name implies, an inn of court in England originally provided accommodation for lawyers practising in the courts. It gradually took on other functions, including the administration, education and regulation of members, but one of its most important functions was to provide a dining hall in which members could meet and eat together. 'Commons' meant a common table, or shared provisions of daily fare where students would dine with senior members of the society and benefit not only from the discussion of legal issues at a time when books were not widely available, but also from the professional gossip exchanged on these occasions. Candidates for the Irish Bar were obliged to keep a minimum number of commons in one of the inns of court in London, and, from the 1780s onwards, at the King's Inns itself.

In the early years of the seventeenth century a fire and explosion at Dublin Castle underlined the need for the courts of justice, then sitting at the castle, to seek safer accommodation.[6] Blackfriars was suggested and appeared to be a suitable location for the building of such courts. But they were not to be built there yet: the citizens of Dublin did not want to see the courts move outside their walled city and promised financial help in refurbishing buildings which stood in the precincts of Christchurch Cathedral (Fig. 1.2).[7] In 1606, while this work was in progress, the courts of justice moved temporarily to Blackfriars.

This probably prompted the judges and lawyers to revive the idea of having, at Blackfriars, a collegiate establishment for the legal profession where they could meet and eat.[8] So in 1607, spearheaded by the judges and by Lord Deputy Arthur Chichester who himself enrolled as a fellow of the society, the King's Inns was revived. Blackfriars was conveyed to the lawyers following the departure of the courts in 1608 'to hold ... forever, with the intent that the judges and professors of the common law in Ireland ... shall have and possess all ... the said premises,

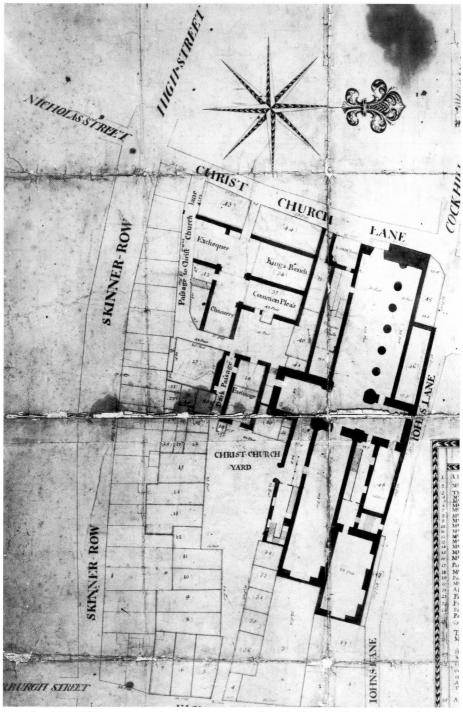

Fig. 1.2 *The courts can be seen on Thomas Reading's map of the Liberty of Christ Church Cathedral, 1761. (Photograph courtesy of the Representative Church Body Library)*

for an inn'.[9] Membership expanded rapidly, repairs were carried out to buildings and by 1609 chambers were ready for allocation to members. The following year chambers were reallocated in favour of those members who would be prepared to carry out without delay necessary repairs and even reconstruction.

Speed's map gives a fairly accurate depiction of the general layout of the site in 1610, with the buildings to the west taking up most of that narrow section of the plot. The building to the left of number '3' on the map is the friars' hall and dortor, or dormitory, where the courts sat between 1606 and 1608. To the west of this is the area which was known as the 'cloysters', an enclosed garden or courtyard around which was a covered walk used by the Dominicans as part of their friary. The south side of the cloister was bounded by a wall, while on the north were some 'auntient stone buildings'.[10]

The 'Black Book' of the King's Inns, which opens with the reorganisation of the society in 1607, is the earliest manuscript in its possession, and it records many cases of lawyers building their own chambers, underlining the fact that the property at Inns Quay was in a bad state of repair. Chambers were 'built' or renovated in the cloister area and in a part of the friars' hall that had been converted to this purpose. It would appear that, at most, only two dozen lawyers had chambers at the King's Inns at any one time and some of these would share in pairs.

Between 1627 and 1629 a new kitchen and a parlour were built. The parlour was located on the ground floor of a building to the north of the hall, with a cellar below and rooms above it. These were probably constructed in anticipation of an increase in membership of the society as Catholics, who had been excluded from the inns since 1613, were now re-admitted.[11] With the arrival of Thomas Wentworth as lord deputy in 1633 more significant building got under way. A court of wards, record offices and chambers were built along the west side of the cloister.[12]

The steward of the society, Randall Beckett (fl. 1633–73), secured a lease in 1638 under which a large portion of the eastern half of the three-acre site beyond the inns' garden (marked 'b' on Stoke's map, Fig. 1.3) passed to him, for development purposes.[13] The granting of this lease would have serious repercussions for the society later. Under its terms Beckett was obliged to keep the inns' garden, and a rather lyrical passage describes how it should be planted:

> … with knottes and borders of sweet herbs, pot herbs, flowers, roses
> and fruit, he finding sufficient pot herbs for the kitchen of the said house

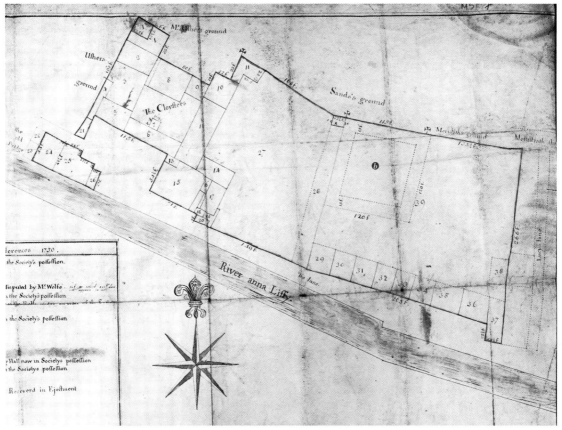

Fig. 1.3   *'A Map of the Ground belonging to the Kings Inns, in the Parish of St Michans Dublin'*
by Gabriel Stokes, 1728.

and strewing herbs for such of the judges and king's counsel as shall be resident in the said King's Inns for the dressing of their chambers in summer.[14]

However, it was stipulated that, in the event of a decision being made to build the courts of justice, the chosen site would be this garden and Beckett would be released from his obligation to tend it. He was also to create and maintain a walled garden forty feet square, to the east of the inns' garden where fruit trees and vegetables were to be planted, and any profit from such produce could be retained by Beckett. This garden was for the use and pleasure of 'such of the judges and king's counsel of the said King's Inns which shall be resident in the said house'. But

5

the main reason for leasing such a sizeable site to Beckett was for him to build and develop the land for the future benefit of the society. Believing him to be a safe pair of hands, as he had overseen the building of a summer-house on the site, the society allowed him to set about building as many houses as he thought fit so long as they were built of brick 'with stone or brick chimneys and covered with slate, tyle or lead'. A member of the society, Beckett had been elected steward in 1633 and from then until 'at least 1657' he pursued, according to Bartholomew Duhigg, the first historian of the King's Inns, a 'mixed career of open impudence or concealed fraud'. For himself and his family, he built a large house on the site that had ten hearths.[15]

In the late 1630s many alterations were made to the main buildings: yet another new kitchen and the summer-house were constructed, and houses were built by many of the lawyers on the society's land.[16] Conditions for the courts of justice at Christchurch had become very cramped and Wentworth's proposal to build the new courts on the site of the inns' garden must surely have encouraged lawyers to acquire their own lodgings close by. These favourable developments were halted by the Rebellion of 1641 and the subsequent arrival of Oliver Cromwell in Ireland. After the Restoration in 1660, construction was resumed on the society's premises, albeit at a much reduced level, while a highly disadvantageous renewal of the lease for sixty-one years was granted to Beckett's son in 1679. The effect of this was to alienate to the Beckett family about one-third of the property of the society for a further 100 years until 1780. In 1661 'the society's butler appears to have been about to pay rent to Randall Beckett for use by the society of part of its own garden'. Moreover, this extension to the lease increased the Becketts' rent from 20s. (agreed in 1638) to only £5 per annum, a paltry increase particularly in relation to the hundreds of pounds per annum which the Becketts received from their sub-tenants (as the society discovered after 1780).[17] In 1660, Beckett's daughter, Hester, had married Richard Reynell, later to be knighted by the lord lieutenant and to become chief justice of the king's bench in 1690. As a member of the society's council Reynell was one of two who in November 1678 were asked to prepare the lease for William Beckett, his brother-in-law. By 1682, according to the Black Book, Reynell too was in possession of a substantial amount of land at Inns Quay on which he built a mansion (see Fig. 1.3, no. 15).[18]

John Dunton, a visitor to Dublin in the 1690s, called the buildings of the King's Inns and the houses built by Beckett along the river front 'a handsom street lyeing upon ye Riva, It has a Cloyster, in which Is [?] a Large hall where ye Judges and other men of ye Law dine in term time at Comons'.[19] Contrary to these appearances, one of the judges complained in 1692 that his lodgings were 'ruinous, requiring new floors, stairs, chimneys, partitions, wainscot and windows glazed'.[20] With the buildings in such bad order it was not surprising that early in the eighteenth century the society began to think about selling all or part of the site so that they could erect new buildings for the society either there 'or in some other convenient place in the city'.[21] Eventually a bill was passed in 1752 granting the society permission to sell or lease its property.[22] However, deeds were lost; rents were ridiculously low; and the trustees in whom the ground was vested by this Act, never made use of their newly won powers.[23] The total annual income to the society from rents on the property between 1753 and 1780 was less than £30.[24] Thus, the society was unable to maintain its property; the buildings continued to decay, and the society to stagnate; and, according to Duhigg, prostitutes and thieves made use of the old chambers there.[25]

From about 1635, buildings at the inns had been used by the government as a repository for parliamentary and judicial records. A report of a committee to inspect the condition of the public records in 1739 found 'the whole Building of the Inns, in a decayed and ruinous Condition'; the ceilings of offices including that of the Rolls Office were propped up to prevent the floors above from collapsing as the timbers were so rotten; and parts of the building were

> ... inhabited by very low poor people ... [where] there are many Fire-
> places, the Hearths of which are ... broken ... also thin Deal-partitions,
> Straw-beds, and other combustible stuff ... If through the Carelessness
> or Villainy of these People, a Fire should break out in any of their
> Chambers ... they would run a manifest Hazard of being burn'd to the
> Ground ...[26]

When in 1756 £5,000 was made available for building new premises for safeguarding the public records, the benchers saw an opportunity to dispose of their property, and they promptly made representations to government stating that they were 'willing to accommodate the public with such part of the said ground as might be necessary ... on reasonable terms'.[27] In 1760 the Crown solicitor approached the society to inquire what rent they were seeking, and 'whether they would have any particular clauses inserted [in the proposed lease]'.[28] It is important to note that there seemed to be no question at this stage that the society would not be compensated for handing over its property. In 1762 the Irish House of Commons resolved 'that the Ground belonging to the Benchers on the Inns-Quay is the most proper Place for building Courts of Justice and publick Offices on'. Significantly, an amendment was passed deleting the words 'Courts of Justice'.[29] It is most likely that the amendment was made in order to placate the citizens of Dublin who again felt threatened by the courts moving across the Liffey.

Fourteen years were to pass before the foundation stone of the public offices was laid on Inns Quay in 1776. The delay was no fault of the benchers who were more than willing to facilitate developments on the site and who had, by 1770, given up any hope of retaining their premises. In June 1771 the benchers urged the lord lieutenant 'that a Repository for the Public Records is extremely wanted and that the most proper Situation for the same will be on Ground on the King's Inns belonging to this Society', and in January 1773 they reassured his Excellency 'of the hearty Concurrence of this Society in an Object of such great National Consequence so long Wanted and so Universally desired'.[30] In 1776, before any agreement had been entered into, 'servants of the crown' entered the premises and 'began to erect the present western range of law offices therein'. The society permitted this incursion because it was still 'relying on the faith of Government, and Parliament, for reasonable compensation'.[31]

---

[1] The Four Courts, designed by James Gandon, now stands on this site at Inns Quay.

[2] According to Maurice Craig, in 1660 the city measured one-ninth of a square mile. Craig, M., *Dublin 1660–1860* (Dublin 1969) p 5.

[3] Kenny, C., 'On holy ground: the benchers and the site of the present Four Courts before 1796', in Costello, C. (ed.) *The Four Courts: 200 Years* (Dublin 1996) pp 2–3.

[4] *S.P. Hen VIII*, iii, 321–2; petition transcribed in Kenny, C., *King's Inns and the Kingdom of Ireland; the Irish 'inn of court' 1541–1800* (Dublin 1991) pp 269–71.

[5] Kenny, C., 'On holy ground', pp 3–4.

[6] Kenny, C., 'On holy ground', p 5.

[7] McParland, E., 'The Old Four Courts, at Christ Church', in Costello, C. (ed.) *The Four Courts: 200 Years* (Dublin 1996) footnote 3; Sir John and Lady Gilbert (eds) *Calendar of Ancient Records of Dublin*, 18 vols (Dublin 1889–1922) Vol. II, pp 478, 501; CARD V, p 377; CARD VI, p 83.

[8] Kenny, C., *King's Inns* (Dublin 1992) p. 73.

[9] Quoted in Kenny, C., 'On holy ground', p 5.

[10] 'Lease of tenement and buildings Inns Court', Trustees of the Inns of Court to George Carleton, 23 June 1654 (KI MS G2/4–7).

[11] Black Book, ff 21r–2v.

[12] Stokes' map, 1728–50, nos 3 and 5 together (KI Map cabinet M5/7).

[13] Lease to Randall Beckett, 2 June 1638 (KI MS G2/4–6).

[14] Quoted in Kenny, C., *King's Inns*, p 114.

[15] Loeber, R., *Architects in Ireland 1600–1720* (London 1981) pp 19–20. According to Loeber, Beckett is mentioned in connection with the building of a fairly substantial summer-house, which may have been known by 1664 as the 'banquetting house'. It can be seen on Stokes' map of 1728/50 at the end of the high-walk at no. 28 and 'a'.

[16] Kenny, C., *King's Inns*, p 114.

[17] Kenny, C., *King's Inns*, pp 115, 145; Black Book, ff 260v–1.

[18] Black Book, ff 261r, 264v, 265r; Ball, F. E., 'Some notes on the Irish judiciary, 1660–1685', *Cork Historical and Archaeological Society*, Vol. VII, 2nd series, 1901, pp 219–21; Kenny, C., *King's Inns*, p 298. Reynell's and Hester's son (then Sir Thomas Reynell) sold a plot of land to Luke Gardiner in 1721, on part of which he built Henrietta Street.

[19] Bodleian Library, Oxford, MS Rawl. D. 71, f 26. My thanks to Dr Edward McParland for this reference.

[20] Power, T., 'The "Black Book" of King's Inns: an introduction with an abstract of contents', *The Irish Jurist*, Vol. XX (1985); Black Book, ff 275r–5v. The hall was in sufficiently good repair in 1718 to hold an auction of paintings and tapestries, advertised in *Pue's Occurrences*, Vol. XV, No. 85, 18–22 November 1718.

[21] Draft of Act 'for selling or leasing certain houses and edifices with their appurtenances commonly called the King's Inns' 1743 (KI MS G1/1–1).

[22] *Commons Journals Ireland*, V, p 107.

[23] *Pamphlets Relating to Ireland*, collected by Haliday, C., Vol. 617, No. 4 (Royal Irish Academy 1792) p 9.

[24] Kenny, C., *King's Inns*, p 229.

[25] Duhigg, B., *History of King's Inns* (Dublin 1806) p 295.

[26] A Report from the Lords Committees 1740, Haliday Collection, Box 194, Tract 2, pp 4, 5, 6, 13, 14, RIA.

[27] King's Inns, *Reports of the Committee Appointed by the Benchers of the Honourable Society of King's-Inns on the 23rd of January 1808* (Dublin 1808) pp 8–9.

[28] Ibid., pp 9–10.

[29] *Commons Journals Ireland*, vii, p 160, pp 170–1.

[30] King's Inns, Admission of benchers 1741–92, pp 130, 135.

[31] King's Inns, Reports of the Committee, 1808, p 12.

TWO HUNDRED AND FIFTY
YEARS AT INNS QUAY

From an architectural point of view, Dublin had grown and prospered greatly by 1776. John Rocque's 1756[1] map of Dublin shows how the city had expanded in all directions, but particularly to the east. The Old Bridge had been superseded to the east by Ormonde Bridge (1680s) and Essex Bridge (1670s, rebuilt 1753); below the latter on the south side was the old Custom House, and further to the east on the same side of the river were Stephen's Green and Sir Edward Lovett Pearce's Parliament House. North of the river were residential areas such as Henrietta Street and Sackville Street. Both streets were laid out by Luke Gardiner, on a portion of whose land the King's Inns now stands.

In the twenty years between Rocque's map and the laying of the foundation stone of the public offices on Inns Quay in 1776, the work of the Wide Streets Commissioners (WSC), which would transform Dublin quite radically, had begun. Established in 1757 by an Act of Parliament 'for making a wide and convenient Way, Street, or Passage, from Essex-bridge to the Castle of Dublin', the Wide Streets Commissioners were soon enabled to extend their powers until the planning of the entire city was under their control: 'They were involved in all, and directly responsible for most, of those features in any early 19th century map of Dublin which differ from Rocque's map of 1757.'[2] One of their earliest projects, *c.* 1765, was to broaden the quayside at Inns Quay. In doing so they pulled down three houses owned by the society, which were built alongside the Old Bridge at the edge of the river, and separated from the main premises by a lane (nos 24, 25, 26 on Stokes' map, Fig. 1.3). A valuation jury awarded the society £506.17s.6d. in compensation but by 1808 the society had no record of having received this payment.[3]

The inscription on the foundation stone of the Public Offices, laid on 25 October 1776, makes no mention of the Courts of Justice. *Faulkner's Dublin Journal* in its report of the ceremony informed its readers that the inscription was for 'a Suit[e] of Buildings containing, the public Law Offices, the Hall and Law Library for the Use of the Society of the King's Inns ...'.[4] The architect was an Englishman, Thomas Cooley (*c.* 1740–1784), who had recently, in 1768, relegated another Englishman, James Gandon (1742–1823) into second place in the competition to design the Royal Exchange, a building that was nearing completion at this stage and that would, together with the Parliament House and the work of the WSC, spearhead the great building boom that took place in Dublin in the second half of the eighteenth century. Cooley sketched a number of ideas for the building, apparently in the dark about what precisely his building was to accommodate and how extensive it should be.[5]

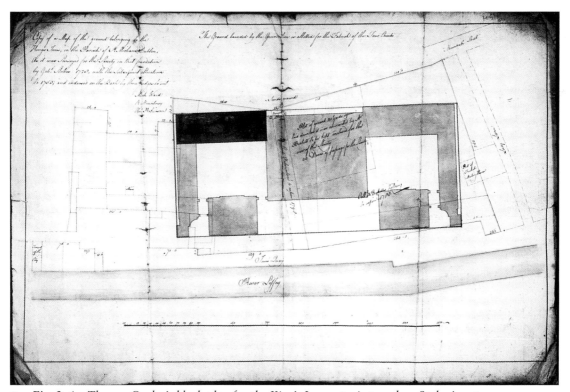

Fig. 2. 1 Thomas Cooley's block plan for the King's Inns superimposed on Stokes' map.

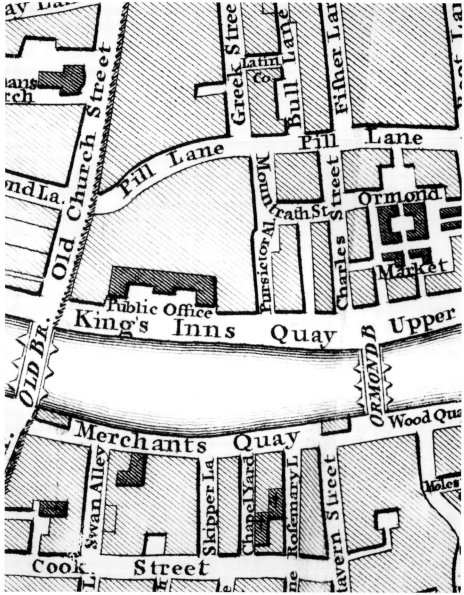

Fig. 2.2   *Cooley's amended plan for the building shown in Pool and Cash's* Views
of the most remarkable public buildings … in the city of Dublin, *1780.*

Superimposed on the copy of Stokes' map of 1728 in the King's Inns library is
a block plan attributed to Cooley on the back of which is written the year, 1776
(Fig. 2.1). Edward McParland has shown that the free-standing block to the front
of the west courtyard and linked to the Records Offices by an arch was to

accommodate the King's Inns.[6] In 1780, Pool and Cash published a block plan of a proposed E-shaped building which tells us that, by then, Cooley had discarded the free-standing blocks to the front and pulled back the central block to create a plan very similar to Gandon's later design (Fig. 2.2).[7] McParland has discussed the similarities in the layout of the central block for the courts as envisaged in a sketch by Cooley[8] and as built by Gandon (Fig. 2.3). This is not to suggest that the genius behind the building of the Four Courts is anyone other than Gandon who had to contend with the difficulty of continuing another architect's work, but to demonstrate that Cooley, like Gandon, was a man of ideas despite his fairly pedestrian design for the public offices (Fig. 2.4).

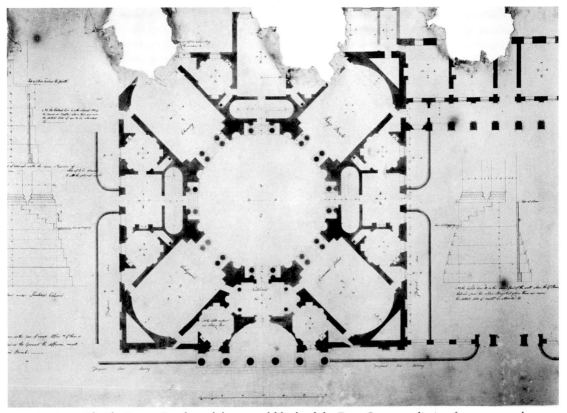

Fig. 2.3　*Plan by James Gandon of the central block of the Four Courts radiating from a central rotunda.*

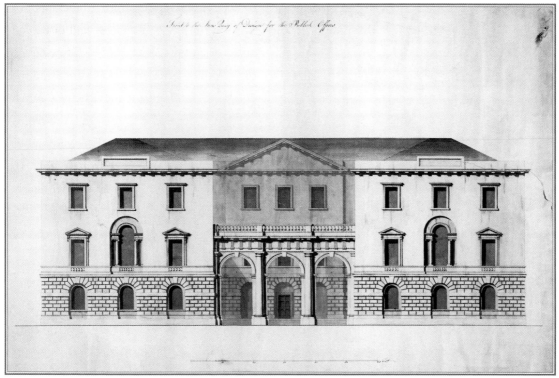

Fig. 2.4 *'Front to the Inns Quay of Design for the Publick Offices' by Thomas Cooley.*

Thomas Cooley died in 1784. By this time the western and northern ranges had been built but the final design had apparently not been decided. Gandon was appointed to succeed Cooley. According to Gandon's biographer, Thomas J. Mulvany, all that remained to be decided in December 1784 was whether the central block should accommodate the Courts of Justice or the King's Inns.[9] Gandon probably started building in 1785 to the design recorded on a signed drawing in the King's Inns library inscribed 'Elevation of The New Courts approved by His Grace The Duke of Rutland 1785'.[10] An Act of Parliament in that year granted £3,000 to the lord chancellor and chief judges 'towards building further offices for the publick records and courts of justice adjoining',[11] and the foundation stone for the new Four Courts was laid on 13 March 1786 by the Duke of Rutland. Those present included the lord chancellor, judges and king's counsel.

Because of the decision to exclude accommodation for the society from the new plan for the Four Courts, Lord Chancellor Lifford, at some time between

1785 and 1789 (when he was succeeded by Lord FitzGibbon, afterwards the earl of Clare), asked Gandon to make designs for a hall for the society 'on the vacant Ground belonging to the Society to the West of the new Courts, together with a Survey of the Houses in Pill Lane and Church Street, that when opportunity offered they might be occasionally purchased and adapted to Chambers, which Drawings are among the Society's papers'.[12] This is recorded in a letter written by Gandon to the benchers in January or February 1804 that has recently been discovered in the archive of the King's Inns. It was found among other unpublished documents which, regrettably, do not include the drawings mentioned. The piece of land west of the Four Courts appears to be the western section of the site occupied by the old King's Inns. This can be seen to the left of the block plan on Figure 2.1. Pill Lane lies along the northern boundary of the site and Church Street lies on its western boundary. From this we can conclude that Gandon was aware of the society's building requirements from the time he took over from Thomas Cooley and that he was providing drawings for them at this early stage.

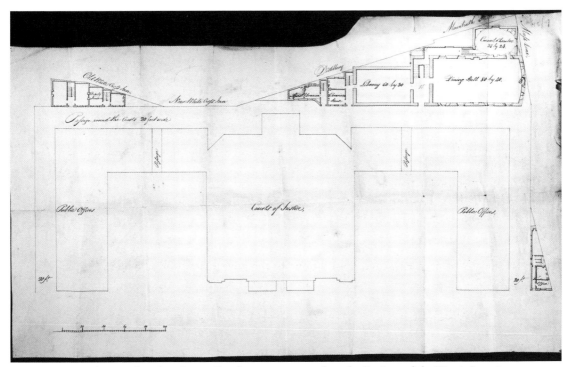

❧ **Fig. 2.5** *Plan attributed to James Gandon to accommodate the Society of the King's Inns in spaces surrounding the Four Courts, 1790.*

In 1790 another plan was drawn up for the construction of buildings for the society, this time in very constricted spaces around the Four Courts (Fig. 2.5.) The plan is unsigned, but a number of factors point to its author being Gandon, not least its handwriting. First, Gandon had already made drawings for the society. Second, there was now a new lord chancellor, Lord Clare who, as an admirer of Gandon, might have asked for new designs and, third, the layout of the accommodation in such a restricted space is well thought out and designed. An oval council chamber fits into an awkward angle to the north of the plan. The dining hall adjoining it has a curved or D-shaped east end and a fireplace on each side. The room was likely to be two storeys high with windows (for light only, as Gandon had an aversion to them) at second storey level.[13] The overall plan is less than ideal with offices for the treasurer south of the main buildings on the river-front, and the accommodation for the deputy treasurer in yet another triangular site to the north-west of the Four Courts. Nothing came of these plans. It is worth noting, however, that the participation of Lord Clare (John Fitzgibbon), who had an exalted idea of both his office and the legal profession, was probably a major factor in the decision to eventually build.[14]

The question of compensation became a thorny one for the benchers as there was a real conflict of interest here. The monies voted by parliament at regular intervals between 1777 and 1794 for the building of the Four Courts were allocated to the lord chancellor and members of the judiciary, and it was the judiciary that controlled the inns. This might explain why the government in 1776 felt sufficiently confident that the society would not prevent them from building on the now derelict site. Things were not looking good for the society by 1790. They had allowed themselves to be squeezed out of their site on Inns Quay without any sign of compensation. They were still careless about looking after their remaining property on the site, and they were without proper accommodation in which 'to meet and eat'. Repeated applications to the government for compensation failed. In February 1794 the only piece of land left in the possession of the society, which lay to the west of the Four Courts, was leased to James Leckey 'for three lives, renewable for ever' at an annual rent of just over £260. Such a rent begs the question of how much the society could have made if, following the expiration of the lease to the Beckett family in 1780, it had purposefully pursued the government for compensation for the site of the courts.

In April 1796 the benchers decided that ejectment proceedings should be taken 'that the Society may not loose so considerable a part of their Property without a reasonable Compensation', but they later changed their minds.[15] The reason may have been reluctance on the part of the benchers to become involved in a public battle with the government over compensation, particularly as the judges had just had their first sitting in the new courts.[16]

The final decade of the eighteenth century saw the society bereft of any land on Inns Quay through its own mismanagement. Like the Dominicans before them, the society was unceremoniously ejected from the site of Blackfriars without compensation or the prospect of it. Unfortunately, the benchers had not yet learned by their mistakes. In 1793–4 they acquired land on Constitution Hill at an exorbitant rent and found themselves once again trying to extricate themselves from a situation created by their own lack of foresight.

---

[1] Rocque, J., *An Exact Survey of the City and Suburbs of Dublin* (Dublin 1756).

[2] McParland, E., 'The Wide Streets Commissioners: their importance for Dublin architecture in the late 18th–early 19th century', *Quarterly Bulletin of the Irish Georgian Society*, Vol. XV, No. 1, January–March 1972, p 26.

[3] King's Inns, Reports of the Committee, 1808, pp 14–15.

[4] *Faulkner's Dublin Journal*, 24–26 October 1776.

[5] Caledon sketchbook, held in a private collection in Ireland. A copy is in the Irish Architectural Archive.

[6] McParland, E., 'The early history of James Gandon's Four Courts', *The Burlington Magazine*, Vol. CXXII, No. 932, November 1980, pp 727–35.

[7] Pool, R. and Cash, J., *Views of the Most Remarkable Public Buildings … in the City of Dublin* (Dublin 1780).

[8] McParland, E. 'The early history of James Gandon's Four Courts', fig. 11.

[9] Mulvany, T. and Gandon, J. jnr (eds) *The Life of James Gandon* (Dublin 1846) p 96.

[10] In the Receipts for Public Monies (KI MS H1/1–2) all of Cooley's signed receipts were for work done on the 'Publick Offices of Records'. From 29 March 1786 Gandon's receipts were for 'Publick Offices and Courts of Justice adjoining'.

[11] *Stat. Ire., 25 Geo. III, c.24.*

[12] Gandon's account book (KI MS H2/1–2).

[13] This plan in some respects anticipates the present dining hall on Constitution Hill.

[14] My thanks to Dr A.P.W. Malcomson for pointing this out to me.

[15] KI Benchers' Minutes 1792–1803, f 92v; Kenny, *The King's Inns*, p 237; King's Inns, Reports of the Committee, 1808, p 13.

[16] KI Benchers' Minutes 1792–1803, f 100v; Kenny, C., 'On holy ground', p 19.

CONSTITUTION HILL –
A NEW BEGINNING?

Without a dining hall or indeed any other accommodation, the benchers in April 1792 ordered the treasurer, William Caldbeck, to 'take the Music Hall in Fishamble street and fit the same for the accommodation of this Society as a dining Hall until one more convenient can be built'.[1] It was in this music hall, incidentally, that Handel's *Messiah* received its first performance in 1742. But the owner of the hall, a Dr Erskine, had deceived the benchers about its condition and the agreement was cancelled. In June Caldbeck was instructed to take the tennis court in Townsend Street and 'fit it up as a temporary hall and library'.[2] Commons were subsequently resumed there.[3] Attendance was high at the beginning and committees were established to 'choose the best claret and port wine', but numbers decreased over the next few years. In November 1797 the hall was flooded and commons were suspended once again.[4]

Meantime, the search for a site on which the society could build an inn continued during 1792 and 1793 and a number of possibilities were inspected. At a benchers' meeting in November 1793 a site, located about one mile north of the new courts, was brought to their attention. It extended from the Linen Hall north to the River Bradoge and from Henrietta Street west to Constitution Hill. Caldbeck was ordered to open negotiations with its 'several proprietors'. This site comprised two adjoining parcels of land, the freehold of which was owned by the dean and chapter of Christ Church Cathedral, and which were let separately to tenants, namely Lord Mountjoy (formerly Luke Gardiner) and John Egan. They were called respectively the Plover Field and the Lord Primate's Garden and they adjoined the houses and gardens of Lord Mountjoy and Primate Robinson, which were located opposite each other at the top of Henrietta Street. The two plots can be seen quite clearly on John Rocque's map of Dublin dated '1756' (Fig. 3.1). The subsequent acquisition of these plots at great expense was to cause further legal problems for the society over the next number of years.

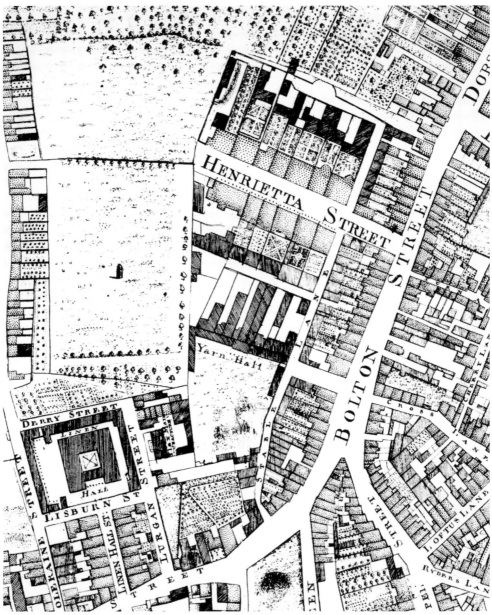

Fig. 3.1 *John Rocque's map shows the adjoining plots of land at the top of Henrietta Street in 1756.*

This was a busy time for William Caldbeck who rose to the challenge with gusto. Called to the Bar in 1755, Caldbeck was a man of wealth and position, whose family owned gunpowder factories in Dublin. He became treasurer to the society in May 1789. Caldbeck fancied himself as an architect and was at this stage harbouring ambitions to design the new inns of court himself. There was nothing particularly unusual about amateur architects in the eighteenth century when many gentlemen dabbled in this art. They would provide the design, have a draughtsman make up the working drawings and entrust the execution of the building to a surveyor or someone who would have the technical knowledge that they lacked.

It appears that 'sometime before' October 1793 Caldbeck was made aware of the Henrietta Street site by John Egan, a bencher of the King's Inns. According to the minutes, Egan acquired the primate's garden on 24 February 1794 for a term of thirty-six years at £420 per annum and three days later on the 27 February leased it to the treasurer for thirty-five years at a rent of £650 per annum.[5] This was looked upon later as a 'monstrous breach of trust'.[6] In the meantime, on 14 December 1793, Lord Mountjoy's trustee, Richard Trench, had let the Plover Field to Caldbeck for thirty-one years at £514 per annum. The two parcels of land together measured just over three acres, and, according to Duhigg, the going rental rate per acre was fifteen guineas.[7] So, for an annual rent of £1,164 the society acquired land which was apparently worth less than £50 per annum.

The rapidity with which agreements were reached for sites that were so obviously over-priced was remarkable. Oddly, there is no record in the benchers' minute book of a meeting taking place between February 1793 and the meeting in November 1793 at which the leases of the Constitution Hill sites were approved, even though at such a crucial time for the society it is difficult to believe that none was held. Caldbeck had plotted his course with care. In 1793 the site subsequently let to Leckey at Inns Quay, as we have seen, was available to the society and would have seemed an obvious place to build. But Caldbeck might have felt that it was too close to the new Four Courts, now in an advanced state of construction, and that the lord chancellor who, together with the Beresford circle, were responsible for bringing Gandon to Dublin in the first place, would put the commission in Gandon's hands. This would not have suited Caldbeck's ambitions, so he leased the site to Leckey in perpetuity, and set about finding another site away from Inns Quay.

On 27 February 1794, the same day that agreement was reached with John Egan for the lease of the primate's garden, Caldbeck produced at a benchers' meeting a plan and elevation of a building proposed by him for the new dining hall and library, which was approved. Caldbeck was in his element. Confident of victory, he had already acquired three new account books bound in leather with a scarlet panel on which were engraved in gold letters his name and the date, 14 December 1793 (Fig. 3.2).[8] Duhigg, librarian to the King's Inns at this period and no fan of Caldbeck, referred sarcastically to 'the transport with which he communicated the intelligence and the satisfaction apparently visible when I hailed him as the legal Vitruvius'.[9]

As soon as Caldbeck had reached agreement to lease Lord Mountjoy's land in December 1793, he purchased padlocks, ropes and a hatchet, and employed a gatekeeper and an 'Inspector of the Works' for the site.[10] By mid-March 1794 preparations had begun in earnest with payments made for gate piers and a porter's lodge; quarry stones had been brought to the site; and Michael Clark and John Forster were paid £50 'on account of Sinking foundations of the new Inns of Courts near Henrietta Street'.[11]

Caldbeck's triumph, however, was short-lived. At a meeting on 7 July 1794 it was ordered that a committee comprising the lord chancellor, the lord chief baron, the attorney-general and bencher Marcus Beresford, together with the treasurer, should be formed 'to consider the Plans and Estimates for the new Hall and Library and what steps are necessary to be taken toward conducting such buildings'. It was further ordered that 'they lay the Plan Elevation and Estimate already furnished before Mr Gandon for his opinion thereon'.[12] This must have been just what Caldbeck would not have wanted. Duhigg describes the proceedings of a subsequent meeting:

> A day was even fixed and nearly approached for laying the foundation stone … I was present at the interesting opposition when a young Bencher, Mr Marcus Beresford, joined to his opinion the strength of an ascendant party. In vain the Treasurer and his partisans pointed out the economy of his approved plan. Why … vary in an expenditure of large amount, and public trust, from the established practice of mankind. … good sense … [persevered], the Treasurer's building party shrunk into a diminished minority, and in that respect blasted his official activity forever.[13]

Not surprisingly, there is no account of this meeting in the minutes or other papers in the King's Inns archive, and Duhigg gives us no date for it. In the meantime, building accounts record payments to workers on the site at Constitution Hill up to mid-August 1794.

We can only speculate as to what happened. Gandon's reaction to Caldbeck's plans was probably unfavourable. Nothing is known of them except that they included 'a projected square' for chambers as well as the dining hall and library, as Duhigg tells us.[14] At the meeting of which Duhigg reports above, Beresford and his circle claimed only that a building of such importance should be entrusted to a 'professed architect', that economy in this case would be 'the harbinger of ruin'. We can assume that Gandon was asked to make drawings for the society for this site, probably after the above meeting, which he then showed to the lord chancellor thereby ensuring that the commission would be his if the drawings met with approval.[15]

By the end of October 1794 about £1,700 had been spent on the preparation of the ground for building. One of the conditions of the lease of the primate's garden was that no building was to be carried out during the lifetime of the primate. After his death in November labourers were paid for over 400 hours' work in the garden, felling trees and pulling down walls. The trees were later advertised for sale. Work had eventually ground to a halt on the site by mid-January 1795.

At about this time the legality of the leases for the grounds from Mountjoy and Egan was called into question. The benchers asked Mountjoy and Egan to release them from their agreements. Of course, having made such an advantageous deal in the first place, they refused.[16] The society sought legal advice on whether or not Egan had acted as a trustee of the society in acquiring his plot but the verdict was not encouraging. The society subsequently decided (in 1795) that it was 'not prudent' to build here and ordered that the Constitution Hill site be advertised to be let or sold, and that the treasurer should look for another site.[17] By November 1795 there were no takers. The society was left with no choice but to remain at Constitution Hill.

The site there measured over three acres. It is situated between the west end of Henrietta Street and Constitution Hill (formerly known as Glassmanoge[18] Road). The site comprised two plots, the Plover Field to the north and the primate's garden to the south, both parts now being joined as one. It is bounded to the south by the Linen Hall, to the north by the River Bradoge which bordered Lord Palmerston's land, and to the east by the houses belonging to Lord Mountjoy and the lord primate. On the Constitution Hill side were houses with gardens, stables, a bakehouse, a racket court, a brewery and various yards. Between the two plots was a passage – 'cart wide' as Duhigg describes it, open between Henrietta Street and Constitution Hill. This passageway has been described as a 'right-of-way', and as a possible reason why Gandon oriented his building at such an odd angle to Henrietta Street. The legal standing of this passageway is not clear, as will be seen later.

At a benchers' meeting on 21 January 1797 a decision was made to advertise ground to be let in lots to members of the society on which they could build chambers to a plan and elevation furnished by Gandon.[19] An Act of Parliament passed in 1798 also embodied the idea of building chambers: it empowered the dean and chapter of Christ Church to grant possession of the site at Constitution Hill to the society forever, so that they might 'build a library, dining-hall and chambers'.[20] When Caldbeck had approached Gandon in February 1798 about the plans for chambers he was told that they were not ready. Chambers were never built at the King's Inns and, as a report of 1808 states, the society received 'a very considerable sum of money from the profession, for the purpose of building Chambers'[21] but that it was spent on 'said ground, upon ... [a] temporary Hall, and other apartments, and in erecting the new Dining Hall, Council Chamber and other buildings', which amounted to 'the sum of £39,700 or thereabouts ...'.[22]

On 8 March 1798, the treasurer was ordered 'to erect a temporary Building at Henrietta street for the accommodation of the Society'.[23] On 11 June, an announcement informing the members of the society 'that a Dining hall and Library have been erected on their ground, between Henrietta Street and Constitution Hill, and that Commons will commence on Thursday the 14th instant', appeared in *Saunder's Newsletter*. This shows that between 8 March and 11 June the temporary building had been erected. As neither plans nor image of this have come to light, one can only speculate from what the building accounts reveal, and these are rather short on detail. Tim McEvoy, described as a carpenter when he worked on the Townsend Street premises and on Caldbeck's aborted building, appears to have been the clerk of works. Payments were made to him from 5 April 'on a/c of building temporary Hall etc. at Henrietta Street' when he received £300, to 27 May 1799 with a payment of £272.16s.10d 'in full of all a/cs for building hall and sundry apartments'.[24] Other payments were made for 'slating and rendering on roofs of the Library, Hall, Kitchen and Offices', for painting and papering, and gravel for walks. The accommodation comprised an entrance hall, dining hall, library, librarian's room, treasurer's room and office, kitchen, and cook's, butler's and porter's apartments. It is safe to conclude then that the building was not made of timber, as one might expect for a temporary erection, but of masonry. Its location was most likely to have been to the north of the site in the Plover Field. It would make sense to use perhaps some of the foundations created for Caldbeck's building, which had to be in the Plover Field area because no building was allowed to take place in the primate's garden as long as the primate lived, and he did not die until November 1794. We know that the temporary building was still standing in 1808 as it is mentioned in a report that year,[25] so it was not inhibiting Gandon's building on the site.

Commons was served in the temporary building up to 1806 when it commenced in the Gandon dining hall.[26] The temporary building remained *in situ* until 1811, when it was sold. Among papers in the King's Inns archive is a statement from 'Davis Auctioneer' advising of a sale by auction at the King's Inns of building materials, at which 'the entire building of the Library, Dining Hall, old Kitchen etc.' was sold for £295.[27]

---

[1] KI Benchers' Minutes 1792–1803, f 2r.

[2] KI Benchers' Minutes 1792–1803, f 7.

[3] Ferrar refers to the society having a 'house near the College-park, in Townshend Street where they meet to dine every day in town', Ferrar, J., *A View of Ancient and Modern Dublin with its Improvements to the Year 1766* (Dublin 1796) p 16.

[4] Duhigg, B., *History of King's Inns*, pp 461, 501; KI Benchers' Minutes 1792–1803, f 89, ff 114, 116, 121, 123.

[5] KI Benchers' Minutes 1792–1803, ff 73–4.

[6] Littledale, W.F., *The Society of King's Inns, Dublin: its origin and progress* (Dublin 1859) p 25.

[7] Duhigg, B., pp 470–1.

[8] KI MS H2/1–/HI/6. Caldbeck was held in sufficiently high esteem by the society that in December 1793 a piece of plate valued at 100 guineas and with an inscription was presented to him 'in testimony of the Sense the Society Entertain of his extraordinary Diligence and merit in Attending to and promoting the Interest of the Society', KI Benchers' Minutes 1792–1803, f 32.

[9] Duhigg, B., pp 475–6.

[10] Building a/cs; Cash expended a/c of the New Inns of Court, Wm Caldbeck (KI MS M1/6).

[11] Caldbeck's building receipts (KI MS M1/7).

[12] KI Benchers' Minutes 1792–1803, f 42.

[13] Duhigg, B., pp 476–7.

[14] Duhigg, B., p 475.

[15] In what looks like a personal notebook of Caldbeck's, marked 'Minutes of Proceedings at the Bench Table', the treasurer notes that 'Mr G had showd [sic] a drawing to Ld Chan' (KI MS B1/6–1).

[16] KI Benchers' Minutes 1792–1803, ff 52v, 64v–7, 70v–7; Duhigg, B., pp 480–1.

[17] KI Benchers' Minutes 1792–1803, f 77.

[18] Sometimes spelled as 'Glasmainoge'.

[19] KI Benchers' Minutes 1792–1803, f 107.

[20] 38 *Stat. Ire.*, *Geo III*, c.49.

[21] The rule of 1793 required every barrister and every attorney to pay a deposit for chambers, which would 'be allowed when the Gentleman shall purchase from the Society, Chambers or Ground to Build Chambers on'. Rules and Orders of the Society of the King's Inns, Rule xxxii (KI MS A2/1).

[22] King's Inns, Reports of the Committee, 1808, p 30.

[23] KI Benchers' Minutes 1782–1803, f 131v.

[24] Receipts Book 1787–99 (KI MS E24/1).

[25] King's Inns, Reports of the Committee, 1808, p 30.

[26] According to *Faulkner's Dublin Journal*, 1 November 1806, p 2.

[27] Sale by Auction of Building Materials, 1811 (KI MS H2/1–5); notice of auction in *The Freeman's Journal*, 13 June 1811.

PERSONALITIES, POLITICS AND PROBLEMS

Once Caldbeck's plans were abandoned it seemed that Gandon, the only *professional* architect mentioned up to now in connection with the building at Constitution Hill, was the obvious choice. Undoubtedly, he was. He had been presenting drawings to the society from the 1780s for the site at Inns Quay, and he states in his letter of 31 January 1804 that he had 'made various designs for a Hall and Library together with plans etc. for chambers for the present site … near Henrietta Street'.[1]

At this point, it is appropriate to take a closer look at Gandon (Fig. 4.1), who dominated the architecture of public building in Dublin from 1781 until his retirement in 1804, just as his Custom House and Four Courts continue to dominate the entire city. Born in 1742 to a Huguenot family resident in London, Gandon took drawing lessons at William Shipley's Academy.[2] In 1757, when he was 15, he joined William Chambers' office in London as an apprentice where he remained until about 1763. The design for the Casino at Marino, Dublin, for Lord Charlemont, was initiated in Chambers' office during Gandon's apprenticeship and its influence can be seen in Gandon's Custom House in Dublin. He

Fig. 4.1   *James Gandon, architect of the King's Inns. Engraving after a watercolour by Horace Hone (1756–1825).*

competed for The Society of Arts premiums and, in 1763, was a prize-winner together with Thomas Cooley. This was the beginning of a rivalry between the two that lasted until Cooley's death in 1784.

It was with Chambers that Gandon's style and approach to architecture were formed, though they were subsequently refined and adapted. McParland says that Gandon is remarkable more for the economy than for the profusion of his ideas.[3] Like Chambers, he preferred Roman to Greek models. His expert handling of masonry details reflects his master's sympathy with France. But Gandon also looked to other architects. Among them he admired the 'movement' in Robert Adam's architecture and imbued his Four Courts with that sense of advance and recess, rise and fall, which enlivens the building. But Adam's style of interior decoration held no interest for him. Another influence was Christopher Wren whose drum of St Paul's dome is invoked at the Four Courts. The end bays of the Four Courts façade, with the treatment of the pilasters, their relationship to the portico, and the shallow, coffered niches, show a debt to the ground-floor bays of the towers on the cathedral's west front. In the King's Inns too the influence of St Paul's is to be seen in the cupola with its paired columns on the diagonal.

Upon leaving Chambers Gandon set up his own practice, and subsequently, with an Irishman called John Woolfe, he published two volumes in continuation of Colen Campbell's *Vitruvius Britannicus* in 1767 and 1771. In the later volume Gandon included his own design for the County Hall at Nottingham, a commission he received in 1768 and his first major work. Drawings for this building demonstrate some of the motifs that are to be seen in Gandon's buildings in Ireland: his aversion to windows and preference for toplighting; screens of paired columns contained between solid bays with niches; the central carved panel flanked by medallions, and the triumphal arch (Fig. 4.2). The plans submitted by him for the competition for the design of Dublin's Royal Exchange in 1769 have been lost but it appears that in the execution of the building, Thomas Cooley, who won the commission, drew upon ideas that had originated in Gandon's plans.

Although Gandon won the first gold medal in architecture to be offered by the new Royal Academy in 1769, his architectural practice was not successful in England, and there was little in his work to suggest the genius who changed the architectural face of Dublin in the closing decades of the eighteenth century. He supplemented his income by publishing and by print-making.

Fig. 4.2 *Section of the County Hall, Nottingham, Gandon's first major commission, which shows some of the motifs used by him in his work in Ireland.*

It is likely that Gandon met the Princess Dashkova, a friend of Catherine the Great of Russia, at artist Paul Sandby's convivial Sunday gatherings in London, called *conversazioni*. She was sufficiently impressed by Gandon to invite him to St Petersburg to build, an invitation he eventually declined. Gandon was a gregarious man who made and kept many friends throughout his life. Sandby took every opportunity to introduce him to influential and well-connected people. Lord Charlemont, whom Gandon had met while in Chambers' offices, was a member of this circle too. At a *conversazione* in 1779 Gandon was introduced to Lord Carlow who subsequently persuaded John Beresford, chief commissioner of the Revenue, that Gandon was the man to design the Custom House in Dublin. Not that Beresford needed much persuasion. What he did need was an architect from outside Ireland to enable him to bring about his coup of moving the Custom House downstream from its existing location beside Essex Bridge. Beresford acted quickly and secretly. When he left London in December 1780 he took with him Gandon's first drawings for the building. Gandon arrived in Dublin on 26 April 1781.

Beresford and his friends Lord Carlow, Frederick Trench and Andrew Caldwell, together with Luke Gardiner, were all Wide Streets Commissioners and so had a hand in all of Gandon's major commissions, which included the Custom

House (1781–1791), the House of Lords extension (1784–*c*.1789), the Four Courts (1785–1802), Carlisle Bridge (1791–1795, rebuilt 1880) as well as many private commissions. The period between 1782 and 1800 was not only a high point politically for Ascendancy Dublin but also architecturally, and was dominated by the work of the Wide Streets Commissioners and of Gandon. Dublin was an exciting, cosmopolitan and elegant city. The Act of Union in 1800 brought anticlimax and, in Gandon's *oeuvre*, this was mirrored by the anticlimax of his King's Inns commission, to which we now return.

Gandon was not alone in drawing up plans for the King's Inns: in 1794–5 at least one other architect and probably more were submitting their plans. A former student of Sir John Soane's, Robert Woodgate (d. 1805),[4] who was working at Baronscourt, the Marquess of Abercorn's house in Co. Tyrone, wrote to his patron on 17 February 1795 explaining that

> The King's Inns Society of Dublin have everything ready to begin to [build?] a new Hall, Library and chambers … and now only wait for a Plan; they have had several but approved of none. I have the site of the Grounds and am now making plans for it.

He goes on to name the members of the building committee that had been set up on 7 July 1794, adding 'the Ld Chancellor [Lord Clare] is the principal and sways the rest'.[5] No mention is made in the benchers' minutes of these or of plans from any architect other than Gandon at this stage. But a recently discovered letter from Luke Gardiner (Lord Mountjoy) to Andrew Caldwell (1733–1808), one of the Wide Streets Commissioners and a barrister, throws some light not only on Woodgate's drawings but also on Gandon's proposals for this prestigious commission.[6] It is dated 24 March 1798, just a short time before Mountjoy was killed in the 1798 rebellion, and reveals that Woodgate's plans were favoured by Mountjoy over those of Gandon:

> I have already seen two plans and elevations; The one by Mr Gandon, which I entirely disapprove of, as I think it would rather be a deformity than an Improvement. The other is by Mr Woodgate, who has corrected the errors in Mr Gandon's plan, or rather drew an original one, without those imperfections, which I object to in the other … Mr Woodgates having laid out his courts and buildings at right angles to the street, the

whole has the appearance of perfect uniformity, and the building in front to the street, which is the principal one, shews to the greatest advantage.

He complained that Gandon's buildings were located at right angles to the site 'without any attention whatsoever to Henrietta Street'. Not having seen Richard Morrison's plans[7] he was unable to comment on them but, 'if he has adhered to the form of the Lot, as Mr Gandon has, I would … reject his design'. According to the letter, Lord Portarlington was in favour of Woodgate's ground plan (rather than his elevations) but Mountjoy expected that 'It will require a great deal of exertion to conquer the Interest that Mr Gandon has with the Society'.

Lord Mountjoy (1745–98) had a vested interest in the building of the inns. He was a resident of Henrietta Street, where he lived in number 10, and it was on his former garden to the west of his house, the Plover Field, that the inns was being built. His grandfather, also Luke Gardiner (d. 1755), had laid out and developed Henrietta Street in the 1730s–1740s. Andrew Caldwell was a highly cultivated man who was greatly interested in architecture. It is altogether understandable that Mountjoy would prefer a building that would have its entrance front terminating the view up Henrietta Street. This wide and elegant street, lined with palatial houses was worthy of such a monumental focal point. It is interesting that he was worried that the society's choice might not be guided by the best motives, that is, the superiority of the design, and recommends some lobbying against Gandon's plans, which seem to be the ones favoured by the society in 1798 at least.

At a benchers' meeting on 23 January 1800 a committee, comprising Lords Clare, Clonmel, Carleton and Yelverton with two others, was appointed to direct and supervise the intended buildings at Henrietta Street. Caldbeck was not included. By the end of January drawings had been submitted by Richard Morrison (1767–1849), by 'Myers' – presumably Graham Myers (fl. 1777–1800) – and by Gandon. No mention is made of Woodgate's. On 13 June Gandon's plans were approved. The benchers recommended that the building should start and the treasurer was ordered to pay him £2,000. Duhigg is rather scathing about this: 'As no premium was given to disappointed candidates, nor their designs ever reviewed the reader will naturally conceive that the approbation was preconcerted, and the Society of Benchers gravely assembled to sanctify such resolution'[8]. The perception seemed to have been that Gandon was the society's choice all along, as Mountjoy had warned.

At the same meeting in June 1800 Caldbeck was instructed to inform Gandon that he should now mark out the ground for the new chambers which 'according to his plan is to be occupied by chambers ... or such part thereof as could at present be applied to that purpose ... and that he prepare Plans and Elevations for such Chambers'. Caldbeck was further instructed to receive proposals from persons willing to take such ground.[9] This idea had been mooted in January 1797. Gandon immediately objected to what amounted to a nightmare scenario for any architect to have 'workmen of different employers working at the same time within the gates and the danger of encouraging combination and rise of wages by setting so much building on foot at once'.[10] The laying of the foundation stone of the King's Inns by the lord chancellor, the earl of Clare, took place on 1 August 1800.[11] It was particularly poignant that on the same day the Act of Union received the Royal assent.

Preparation of the site started at once. Just as Gandon favoured certain architectural motifs in his work, so he brought with him to King's Inns his by-now familiar and favoured workmen: stonecutter Frederick Darley, bricklayer John Semple, smith John McKenzie (McKenzie & Mallet) and sculptor Edward Smyth. Richard Louch was the clerk of works. Darley utilised almost £400 worth of ashlar and sand which was already on the site (from Caldbeck's aborted building). A road was cleared to the houses of the librarians who had apparently appropriated dwellings on site at Constitution Hill as soon as the temporary building went up.[12]

At a meeting in June 1802 Gandon's plans for chambers were submitted for approval. A committee was formed to examine the plans, decide how much ground they needed to purchase to enable them to build chambers, and what finance was required for this. As will be seen, this is the first indication for Gandon that not all of the ground necessary for his plan of chambers was in the possession of the society. Duhigg believed that Caldbeck, now a member of the new committee, was behind this deception:

> The situation of the western side was entirely unknown to the architect, who conceived it to belong to the Society, or to be reducible to immediate possession by the nature of its tenancy. Under this impression, the front has been moved so far to the westward as to

approach within a few yards of cowhouses, a Racket Court, and a few obscure tenements inhabited by the poorest class of people.[13]

This refers to dwellings along Constitution Hill, a number of which, on the southern half of the site, were occupied by tenants of the society, and on the northern half to a large plot that was in the possession of Richard Wilson, on part of which was a racket court. This plot came into the possession of the society in only 1833 (Fig. 4.3).[14] By July the committee had decided against purchasing more land, but to build on such land as they did possess according to the plan.

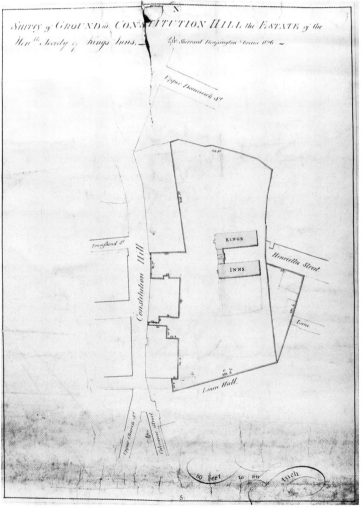

Fig. 4.3   Large blocks of buildings along the Constitution Hill boundary can be seen in Sherrard Brassington Greene's map of 1826.

The plan for chambers submitted at this meeting is likely to be the one described in detail by Duhigg:

> An oblong inclosure, including the western front may be built round the New King's Inns, which will contain twenty-two houses, and form an elegant interior of 497 feet by 224; each house may be fifty-three feet eight inches in front, by thirty-seven feet six inches, and from three to four stories high, with apartments underground. This plan gives six rooms on each floor; the landing leads to a small lobby, a door from which encloses three apartments. The above houses will have rears. But if the adopted plan be to build Chambers without such conveniences, nine additional houses may be erected on the south and north sides. Should Glasmainogue Road be entirely excluded from the intended interior, an iron railing is to form the western boundary.
>
> A plan of one house has been given in and is estimated to build for *five thousand five hundred pounds*, thus, *one hundred and twenty one thousand pounds* would be required to build the square.[15]

Using these dimensions, Hugo Duffy in his book made a plan of the proposed square of chambers, with an elevation and a ground-floor plan of one of the houses. The measurements given by Duhigg, he says, perfectly fit twenty-two sets of chambers around a square.[16]

Gandon informed the building committee on 29 December 1803 that large sums of money were required for finishing the building, and that several tradesmen were owed money for work already done.[17] He was requested to furnish them with a report on the progress of the building together with a financial statement to date. They also required

> … a full and clear Estimate of the money that will be necessary for the Completion of the Dining-Hall of the Society pursuant to his plan thereof, and also for the [sic] putting the building intended for a Library into the best possible state of security and preservation.

Gandon's reply is illuminating.[18] He states that he received only £2,000 for the works in the first year (1800), and received no sum exceeding £3,000 for either of the ensuing years. He makes the point that these

... sums never were sufficient to enable him to conduct a building of such consequence, with advantage to the Society or Credit of the Architect, because the Artificers were greatly restrained and checked in their exertions for want of sufficient advancements of money for the purchase of materials, they having very short credit from the respective dealers ...

He further states that he brought this to the attention of the committee at their meeting in June 1802:

... at which meeting the Right Honble Committee as well as your Architect were first informed, that all the Ground as shewn in the general plan for the Chambers did not belong to the Society. Your Architect then received directions to adopt a plan to the present limited circumstances of the Ground in their possession, which he accordingly did. It was at this meeting your Architect was likewise informed of the situation of the Society's money concerns, which caused him to alter the manner of conducting the works from the usual practice of carrying the walls regularly round and up to a level, that all might settle equally. As the Society's finances would not admit the advancement of a sufficient sum for the above purpose, your Architect conceived it most prudent to direct all his attention to compleating of the wing for the Eating Hall, and that the Council chamber might at a moderate expence be adapted for a temporary Library.

Gandon adds that 'if proper advances of money are made' the building should be completed by May 1805. By the summer of 1802, however, the whole building must have been well under way. It appears that after the above meeting in June 1802, work on the library stopped and Gandon concentrated on completing the dining-hall wing.

One of the most fascinating aspects of the minutes of the meeting in December 1803 is that the society had 'proceeded on the works now in progress on plans of the buildings furnished by Mr Gandon *unaccompanied with Estimates of the expence of erecting them*'[19] (author's italics), a procedure that was now felt to be 'highly unsatisfactory'. This was despite the fact that Lord Avonmore, who signed the minutes of the December 1803 meeting, had sat on the building committees in 1794 (when Robert Woodgate mentioned him in his letter to Lord Abercorn) and in 1800 when Gandon's plans were approved.[20] It was no wonder that by the beginning of 1804 the society found itself seriously short of funds and unable to continue executing the plans in their entirety.

In the abstract that accompanied the letter to the committee, £14,164 had already been paid to tradesmen and £4,594 was still outstanding. In the same document on 16 February 1804, Gandon estimates the cost of completing the dining-hall wing and, 'putting the Building intended for a Library into the best state of security and preservation' at £8,813.[21] In a separate statement of accounts dated 7 July 1804, the estimated cost of finishing the library wing is given as 'at least' £20,000, and the building of chambers at £60,000, a figure based on ten houses being built.[22]

In April 1804 Gandon supplied a variety of estimates for the building of chambers: the cost per four-storey house would be £5,387; if the attic storey were dispensed with, a deduction of £623 would be made. To build the shell only would cost £2,710, and a deduction of £151 would be made if the attic storey were omitted.[23] As part of the same document, the architect sets out a 'Scheme for Setting', or letting, the chambers. In this he states that 'The Ground now in possession of the Society would occupy ten of these Houses', a much-reduced plan from that described by Duhigg in which were twenty-two sets of chambers. The proposed income per house per annum would amount to £300. Of course, as chambers were never built, these figures were all hypothetical, but they demonstrate that Gandon was doing his best to facilitate the society's financial position.

Another important factor for Gandon in his disenchantment with the progress of work at the inns was that the committee to which he reported was very different in 1802 to that of 1800. The lord chancellor, Lord Clare, who died in 1802, was replaced by John Mitford, Lord Redesdale, who visited the site regularly, leaving written complaints for the architect, particularly with regard to the delays in erecting the building. By April 1804 many of Gandon's patrons were dead. Another member of the group, Chief Justice Lord Kilwarden, together with his son-in-law, had been murdered during the Robert Emmet rising in July 1803,[24] and John Beresford, who had retired from the Revenue Board in 1802, had little reason to be in Dublin. Gandon found himself without the support he had enjoyed for his twenty-three years in Dublin; complaints from the lord chancellor and from the committee at the King's Inns about money and delays had made his situation untenable. He submitted a letter of resignation to Lord Redesdale, handing over responsibility for the work to his assistant Henry Aaron Baker.[25]

The letter makes sad reading; he defends his workmen, and himself, and concludes:

> I hope I may be allowed, without the appearance of vanity, to assert, that the works already erected under my inspection, in Dublin, are equal in magnitude and importance to any construction in this part of the United Kingdom, and I trust I have conducted them with credit to myself, as well as satisfaction to those who honoured me with their confidence, and I cannot but regret the misfortune of my not being enabled to give equal satisfaction to your Lordship. Under this impression, I consider it my duty to decline being any longer employed as architect to the King's Inns, and I am convinced that your Lordship will adopt such speedy measures for completing the works as may be necessary.

The letter, as it appears in his biography, is undated.[26] Gandon had written to the Board of Works on 22 March 1804, on which date he wrote tendering his resignation as 'Architect to the Law Courts and Offices', and informing them that he had already notified the lord chancellor of his decision.[27] This resignation as architect to the King's Inns was likely to have been received by the society in December of that year, or January 1805, at which time he sent a final account of monies owed to him and to his workmen. At a meeting on 23 January 1805 it is ordered 'that Mr Gandon's account be referred to the committee and a further Bench meeting on 9th February'. At the February meeting it was decided that 'Artificers and Tradesmen' be paid as the treasurer 'shall think proper and that Debentures be sold out or given to Tradesmen in payment.'[28] There is no further mention of Gandon in connection with building at King's Inns from this date in the minutes, nor, for that matter, is Henry Aaron Baker mentioned at all.

King's Inns was the last of Gandon's great public buildings in Dublin. He retired, aged sixty-two, to his home in Lucan, where he wrote of his experiences, enjoyed his garden and retained his interest in the arts through his involvement with the Royal Dublin Society where he sat on a number of committees. He died in his eighty-second year on Christmas Eve 1823, and was buried in Drumcondra churchyard beside his friend the antiquarian Francis Grose.

[1] Gandon's account book (KI MS H2/1–2).

[2] The information on Gandon's life and work in this section is based on *James Gandon Vitruvius Hibernicus* (London 1985) by Dr Edward McParland, to whom the author is grateful.

[3] McParland, E., *James Gandon*, p 7.

[4] Woodgate, a carpenter turned architect, worked mainly in Ulster. He succeeded Vincent Waldre as architect and inspector of civil buildings with the Board of Works in Ireland in 1802 and died in his third year in office. He was succeeded in the post by Francis Johnston (1760–1829).

[5] Abercorn papers, D/623 Mic/18/6, Letters from George Knox to Marquess of Abercorn 1795. Public Record Office Northern Ireland.

[6] From Mountjoy (illegible address) to Andrew Caldwell, 24 March 1798. Private collection (with thanks to Jane Meredith).

[7] Sir Richard Morrison (1767–1849), born in Cork and set up practice in Clonmel. Moved to Dublin about 1800 where he established a flourishing practice specialising in the design of country houses and villas. His son, William Vitruvius, joined his practice in 1809.

[8] Duhigg, B., p 508.

[9] KI Benchers' Minutes 1792–1803, ff 161–2.

[10] Ibid., f 162.

[11] KI Benchers' Minutes 1792–1803, f 163.

[12] The librarian was Stephen Dickson who had taken up his appointment in 1793.

[13] Duhigg, B., p 510.

[14] Book of maps of the estates of the Dean and Chapter of Christ Church Dublin. MSS 2789–90. National Library of Ireland. Book I, f 21, f 89, and Book II, f 52, f 116.

[15] Duhigg, B., p 512.

[16] Duffy, H., *James Gandon and His Times* (Kinsale 1999) p 242.

[17] Gandon's account book (KI MS H2/1–2).

[18] Ibid. This is undated, but the abstract annexed to it is dated 31 January 1804.

[19] Ibid.

[20] Barry Yelverton was raised to the peerage in 1795 and became Viscount Avonmore in 1800.

[21] Gandon's account book (KI MS H2/1–2).

[22] 'Account of the money already expended in building Inns of Court and an estimate of Future Expenditures necessary to compleat the Dining-hall Wing and putting the Building partly erected and intended for a Library into the best state of preservation till the Society shall be enabled by an increase of funds to proceed in finishing the same', 7 July 1804. No. II (KI MS, M7/2, Map drawer 7).

[23] The plan that accompanied this has not been found. Gandon's account book (KI MS H2/1–2).

[24] Robert Emmet (1778–1803), Irish nationalist, organised a rising to be led by him which ended in a scuffle in the streets of Dublin in July 1803. He was captured, tried and convicted, and made a powerful speech from the dock that has ensured his immortality.

[25] Mulvany, T. and Gandon J., *Life*, pp 216–19.

[26] The *Life* intimates that it was in 1806–8.

[27] Minute Book I 1802–1804, Board of Works, 23 March 1804.

[28] KI Benchers' Minutes 1804–19, f 3v; 'Abstract of the Sums of Money due to the Artificers &c &c on Account of the Buildings of the Inns of Court', dated January 1805, Gandon's account book (KI MS H2/1–2).

THE 'TEMPLE'[1]

The building as we see it today is not as Gandon designed it: a wing was added to each side in the mid-nineteenth century, which distorts the balance and harmony of the original (Fig. 5.1). Gandon's plan is curious (Fig. 5.2): two parallel ranges, that on the left for the dining hall and on the right for the proposed library (now the Registry of Deeds), linked by another, narrower range at the west front, rather like a bridge, the ground floor of which is an arcade with three openings. On top of this connecting range is a domed columnar cupola. The cupola, crowning as it does a tripartite façade with columnar centre and pedimented end blocks echoes the description of the Parliament Street façade of Gandon's entry for the Royal Exchange competition.[2] From the arcade it is possible to enter either range by means of side doors or, if preferred, one can make a grand entrance through the doorways flanked by Portland stone caryatids on the west front. The plan bears a striking resemblance to the main block of Worcester College, Oxford (rebuilt between 1720 and 1786) which also has a pair of parallel ranges which contain the chapel and hall respectively, and are linked by a gateway at the west front.[3] While it is possible that Gandon was familiar with this building, there is no evidence to suggest that it influenced his design for the King's Inns.

According to his biography, the design for the King's Inns was 'a favourite study' of Gandon's and indeed his favourite motifs reappear: the ground-floor triumphal arch, his dislike of windows, the cupola already mentioned, derived from Wren, and his use of sculpture. But on no other building has Gandon raised his order to rest upon a rusticated base.[4] His decoration is always elegant and understated. Eschewing for the most part the 'applied' style of Adam's ornament, he relied more on the decorative effects achieved by light and shadow in his use of

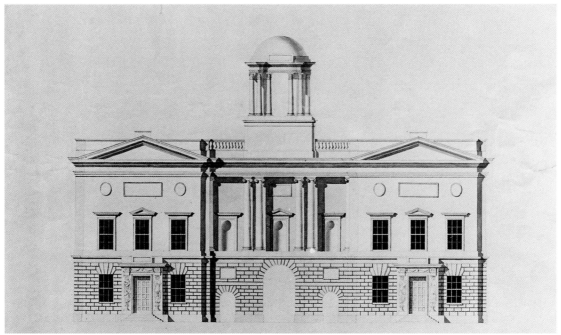

🙠 **Fig. 5.1** *James Gandon's elevation of the King's Inns. (Courtesy of the Irish Architectural Archive)*

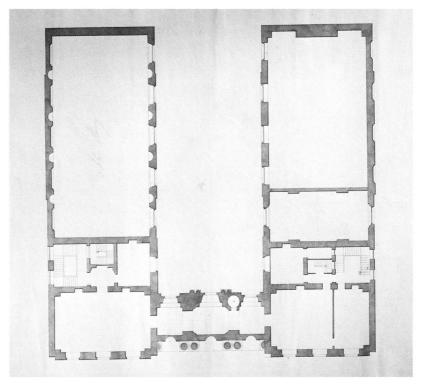

🙠 **Fig. 5.2** *The King's Inns: first-floor plan by Gandon & Baker, 1805. (Murray collection, Irish Architectural Archive. Courtesy David Davison)*

niche, arch, string course and vaulting.[5] His use of sculpture is never arbitrary. He said of the Custom House sculptures that 'an endeavour is aimed at to give them a just character applicable to their destination'.[6] This is true of the sculpture both inside and on the façade of the King's Inns and of the marvellous caryatid doorways, surely unique in Dublin at the time (Fig. 5.3). Edward Smyth (1749–1812), who had carved the sculptures on the Custom House and at the Four Courts previously, was responsible for most of this work. While his multi-figural low-relief compositions lack clarity at the King's Inns, Smyth is undoubtedly at his best with the large figures that enhance and enliven the façade. He charged seventy guineas each for carving '2 caryatid figures in Portland stone each seven and half feet high with Frieze etc. for Entrance into Great Dining-hall' in July 1805.[7] Appropriately, they represent Ceres, goddess of agriculture, holding a cornucopia and, holding a goblet, a Bacchante, a female follower of the god of wine. No payment is recorded for the two caryatids on what is now the Registry of Deeds wing, but a payment was made to his son and assistant John Smyth (c. 1773–1840), for £100 in 1816. No details of this are given. Edward is generally credited with all four caryatids but John may have executed the second pair. They would not have been placed on the building before it became the Registry of Deeds in 1814.[8] The figure representing 'security' holding a key and scroll would be highly suitable for a repository of public records, particularly in view of how these records had been stored previously; the figure symbolising 'law' could be equally interpreted as the keeping of records.

The impressive doors lead into the vestibule of the dining-hall building which is three bays wide, with a Portland stone-flagged floor and vaulted ceiling similar to that in the north loggia of the Custom House (Fig. 5.4).[9] A flight of steps opposite the entrance leads to the dining hall. A drawing in the Irish Architectural Archive suggests that this flight did not emerge into the vestibule as it does now, but was contained between the two walls leading to the dining hall (Fig. 5.5). However, from a recently discovered drawing made by Frederick Darley (1798–c. 1873) in 1846 it appears that, as built, the steps did emerge, but as a series of segmental curves spilling into the space (see Fig. 6.10).[10] This had the effect of disturbing the spatial flow of the vestibule. However, even with this protrusion the vestibule, devoid of applied ornament, has a strongly architectural quality.

🕮 ***Fig. 5.3*** *Main entrance to dining hall flanked by giant Portland-stone caryatids carved by Edward Smyth.*

Fig. 5.4   The vestibule with its Portland-stone floor and vaulted ceiling similar to that in the north loggia of the Custom House.

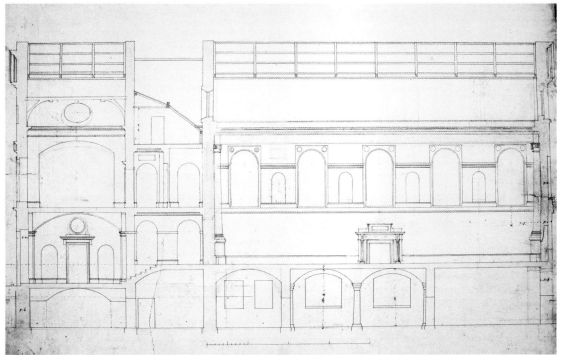

Fig. 5.5   Gandon's section shows an original intention for the short flight of steps from the vestibule to the dining hall. (Courtesy of the Irish Architectural Archive)

⚜ **Fig. 5.6** *The dining hall, the only large public interior by Gandon to have survived in Dublin.*

The building of the extension in 1846 and other alterations over the years, which included enlarging the staircase leading to the first floor, and altering completely the Council Chamber (now the benchers' room), have resulted in the dining hall (Fig. 5.6) being the only large public Gandon interior to have survived (almost intact) in Dublin as both the Custom House and the Four Courts were damaged extensively during the civil war in 1921 and 1922 respectively and required almost complete reconstruction. The late Conor Griffin, a member of the King's Inns and an architectural historian, took issue with this point. He made the suggestion that the dining hall was not completed to Gandon's plans, as he would

⚜ **Fig. 5.7 (opposite)**
The west end of the dining hall. The four brass gasoliers were probably put in place by Frederick Darley.

   Fig. 5.8   *View of the King's Inns from the bottom of Henrietta Street.*

never have sanctioned south-facing windows, given his dislike of windows in general. Further, Griffin believed it odd that the expensive *oeil-de-boeuf* windows on the exterior of the building are ignored on the inside.[11] These are valid points, but if it had been Gandon's intention to have blind windows on the dining hall (to correspond with the library building which would need light), then a different ceiling would have been required to allow light from the *oeil-de-boeuf* windows into the hall.[12]

McParland observes that the east end of the dining hall with its Ionic reredos, where the benchers sit at table on a dais, 'strikes a faintly ecclesiastical note',[13] a remark underlined by a comparison with the interior of the Royal Naval College chapel at Greenwich. The chapel was designed by James 'Athenian' Stuart, possibly with Gandon who worked in partnership with him for a brief period in about 1779/80 when the chapel was being built. Apart from its obvious similarity to the King's Inns dining hall, it contains a number of motifs used by Gandon in his Irish buildings.[14]

Edward Smyth's work can also be seen in the hall where he provided, in stucco this time, the four 'emblematical figures … in the proportion of $7\frac{1}{2}$ ft high in Alto Relievo @ 25 guineas each'.[15] They are placed in pairs over the entablature at each end of the hall (Fig. 5.7).

The question of the King's Inns' orientation, with its back set determinedly to Henrietta Street, the most fashionable street in Dublin in 1800, and its west front facing Constitution Hill (indeed, in 1800 it faced the rears of tenements on Constitution Hill) is often remarked upon. And why build on an apparently cramped space when there was no shortage of land around it?[16] The present arched gateway designed by Francis Johnston in the 1820s at the top of Henrietta Street helps to effect a transition from the street to the inns at this awkward junction, but one has to agree with Lord Mountjoy: Gandon's plan does 'disfigure the approach through Henrietta Street', and if he intended his courtyard as a continuation of the street, he plainly failed (Fig. 5.8). The courtyard is narrow and dark, and one has to walk through it from the street to enter the building from the front. It appears that the laneway had been used by the public up to the time of the King's Inns' purchase of the land.[17]

McParland proposes that the reason might lie in the 'right-of-way' or thoroughfare across the site. This was a narrow passageway 'cart-wide' or 'eleven foot wide' as variously described (notwithstanding the difference in measurement between the two), from Henrietta Street to Constitution Hill, and it divided the Plover Field from the Lord Primate's Garden. The line of the passage can be seen on Rocque's map (see Fig. 3.1, Chapter III). The courtyard between the two ranges follows this passage roughly through the arcade. The precise status of this 'right-of-way' has never been determined satisfactorily, even by the society.

There is no evidence to suggest that a right-of-way was under discussion either at benchers' meetings or with Gandon, unless it was simply understood by all concerned that this facility had to be maintained for the public. Yet this ancient right-of-way does not exist today nor has it since the 1830s when the society demolished the remaining houses fronting Constitution Hill. At this time the ground in front of the King's Inns was levelled, the right-of-way or laneway disappeared, and two new gateways were erected at Constitution Hill, one to the north, the other to the south of the site, as at present. If the route of a right-of-way is so sacred that a building has to be oriented to facilitate it in 1800, how can that route be diverted so easily thirty years later?

But another reason why the building is oriented in such a way involves literally looking at it from a different viewpoint, that is from Constitution Hill. As Mountjoy said in his letter to Caldwell, Gandon set his building at right angles to the site itself. When seen from Constitution Hill, it makes perfect sense: the building would constitute the focal point of one side of a square of chambers, as described by Duhigg. What we see today is only part of a greater scheme.

A drawing of the King's Inns by the architect Francis Johnston (1760–1829) published in 1813 (Fig. 5.9), shows the west front facing a line of buildings which recedes in a concave line opposite the inns itself. It is inscribed 'The Intended line

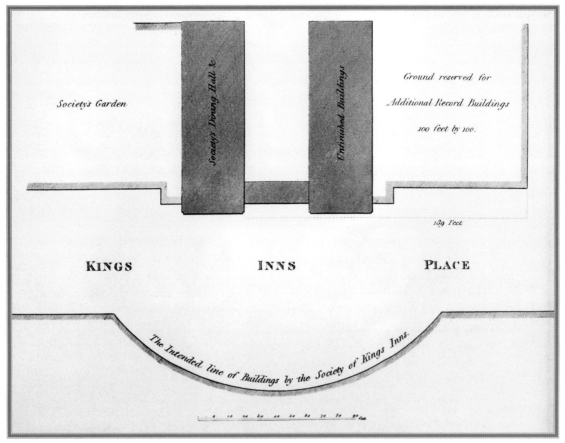

  Fig. 5.9   *Francis Johnston's plan shows the proposed location of chambers.*

of Buildings by the Society of King's Inns'. Such a layout again makes sense of the main front facing westwards, addressing the internal approaches, as McParland points out, and is natural for the dining hall and library to turn their backs on Henrietta Street.[19]

1 Gandon's building on Constitution Hill has in the past been frequently referred to as the 'temple'. It is not clear whether this refers to the temples or inns of court in London, or to the land owned by Lord Palmerston (family name Temple) next to the King's Inns on which Temple Cottages now stand.

2 McParland, E., 'James Gandon and the Royal Exchange Competition 1768–69', *JRSAI*, Vol. CII (1972) p 67.

3 Royal Commission on Historic Monuments England Series, *An Inventory of the Historical Monuments in the City of Oxford* (London, 1939) p 124. My thanks to Dr Edward McParland for drawing my attention to this.

4 McParland, E., *James Gandon*, p 170. Dr McParland gives a detailed description of the building in his book.

5 Ibid., p 173.

6 Mulvany, T. and Gandon, J., *Life*, p 78.

7 Gandon's account book (KI MS H2/1–2) p 68.

8 *Faulkner's Dublin Journal* of 1 November 1806 describes only those on the dining hall, and in their book, Warburton, J., Whitelaw, J. and Walsh, R., having described the decoration on the outside of the benchers' wing, remark that the 'unfinished wing will be completed in a correspondent manner', *The History of the City of Dublin*, 2 vols (London 1818) p 1020.

9 McParland, E., *James Gandon*, p 172.

10 'Articles of Agreement for making Alterations in the Stair Case and Dining Hall of the Society of King's Inns' (KI MS G2/6–5).

11 Griffin also pointed to the type of Diocletian east window that manifests itself as an oval in the interior as evidence of a change in the design. Letter from Conor Griffin to Mrs Camilla McAleese, under-treasurer at the King's Inns, dated August 2002.

12 See IAA Murray Drawings Collection, Drawings by James Gandon and Henry Aaron Baker 'Section of the Great Dining Hall'.

13 McParland, E., *James Gandon*, p 174.

14 Lewis, L., 'The architects of the chapel at Greenwich Hospital', *Art Bulletin*, Vol. XXIX, December 1947, pp 260–7.

15 Gandon's account book (KI MS H2/1–2) p 68.

16 McParland, E., *James Gandon*, p 167.

17 Registry of Deeds, memorials of leases, 14 December 1793 (472/387/302870) and 27 February 1794 (484/100/304532).

18 *Public Records of Ireland Reports 1810–1815* (1813–15) Plate XVIII.

19 McParland, E., *James Gandon*, p 168.

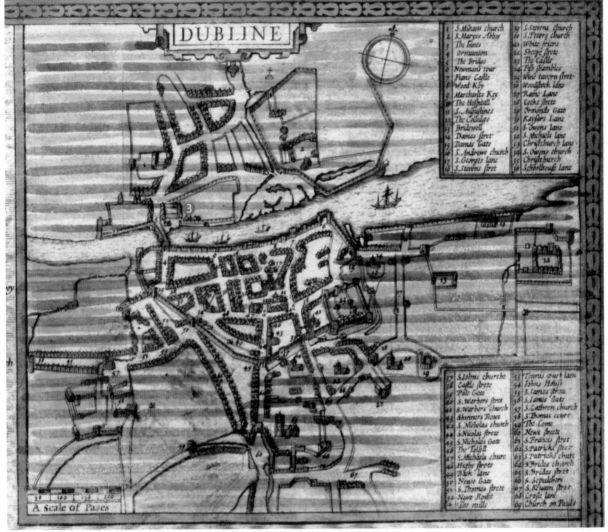

✤ **Fig. 3.2** *One of the engraved ledgers acquired by the treasurer, William Caldbeck, as he commenced building the inns to his own design in 1793.*

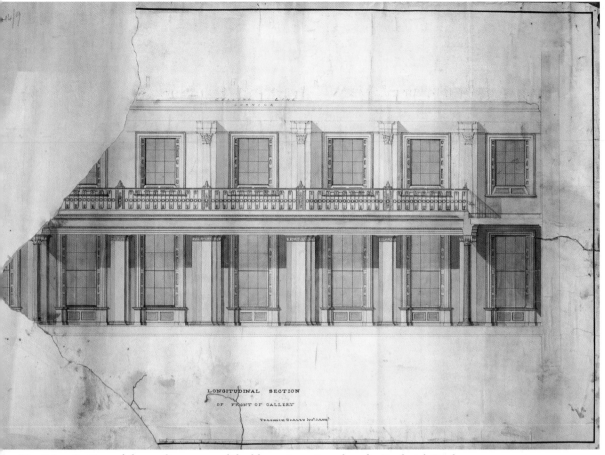

CEILING LINE
CORNICE

LONGITUDINAL SECTION

OF FRONT OF GALLERY

FREDERICK DARLEY JUN'R A.R.H.

Fig. 7.2 *Section of the reading room of the library in watercolour by Frederick Darley.*

✎ **Fig. 7.3 (opposite page)**
The library of the King's Inns in Henrietta Street.

✎ **Fig. 7.5 (above)**
The imposing double height reading room is a superb example of a Greek Revival interior.
(© Tim Imrie/Country Life Picture Library)

Fig. 9.2 *Watercolour of the King's Inns by Raymond McGrath, 1941. The plaster facing and decorative details of the gable end of the building were not replaced in the 1960s when major repairs were carried out to the building. (Courtesy of the Irish Architectural Archive)*

Fig. 9.3 *Original wallpaper, discovered in a ground-floor office in the library in 1997, probably dates to the 1820s.*

Figs 9.4 and 9.5
The restored faux bois wallpaper, and a close-up of a detail. (© Tim Imrie/Country Life Picture Library)

AFTER GANDON

The dining-hall wing progressed slowly towards its completion. Among the last items to be fitted were the three chimneypieces in the dining hall. Darley in 1806 supplied 'Three large Kilkenny and Dove marble chimneypieces, with Dove marble slabs to do. compleat' for £205.[1] The chimneypiece behind the benchers' dais is presumably as supplied, but the other two, on the north and south sides have, instead of the marble slab at their centres, a panel on which is the motto of the society, *Nolumus Mutari* – 'We do not wish to be changed'.[2] The cast-iron surrounds have applied animals and arms in brass decorating them. From payments in the accounts it would appear that these two surrounds came from the hall in the temporary building and were removed from there to their present location (Fig. 6.1).[3]

At last, on 1 November 1806, Faulkner's Dublin Journal reported that:

The wing of the building belonging to the Honourable Society of King's Inns, which was so many years ago begun to be erected ... and which contains the great dining hall, is just finished, so as for the Society to be entertained at dinner there, and to keep their Commons in the ensuing Michaelmas Term.

The writer of the article, who admires the 'handsome' architecture, points out that the 'barely erected' dining hall is only a part of the plan 'and the Society complain of their funds being exhausted; if so they cannot even keep pace, with the hitherto *snail's pace* with which that building has reared its head'. It is also pointed out that for considerably less than the money 'injudiciously and improvidently

☙ **Fig. 6.1** *The fire surrounds on two of the three chimneypieces in the dining hall are of iron with brass ornaments of fasces and helmets, above which a lion and a hound flank a large tablet bearing the society's motto in an open book.*

☙ **Fig. 6.2** *A drawing from Francis Johnston's office may indicate the state of the building c. 1812. (Courtesy Irish Architectural Archive)*

already expended upon that piece of ground, an handsome edifice adequate to all its purposes might have been many years since completed.' The writer bemoans the condition of the site surrounding the hall, prophesying that it is 'long to stand surrounded by rubbish, ruins, and unfinished foundations; which most probably the grandson of the youngest man living shall never see completed ...'.

Thankfully, it did not take quite as long a time as the writer in the *Journal* expected. Six years later in 1812 the condition of the site was being actively considered. It was obviously an eyesore, with an unfinished building and various materials lying around, not to mention the tenements on the Constitution Hill side (Fig. 6.2). Francis Johnston who succeeded Gandon as Ireland's most important

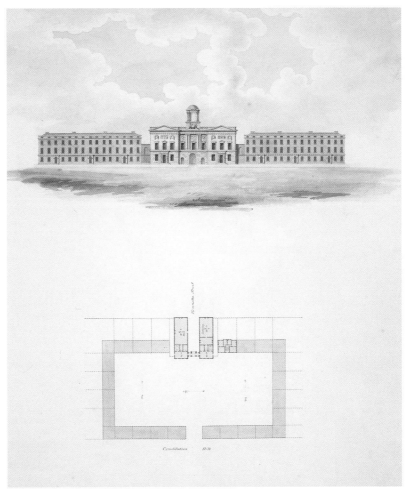

❦ *Fig. 6.3*   *Proposed elevation and plan for a square of chambers, with Gandon's building as its centrepiece, possibly by Gandon's partner Henry Aaron Baker, or from Johnston's office. (Private collection)*

architect, laid plans before the benchers for improving the grounds and the buildings. One of those may have been a plan and elevation that shows a square of chambers of three storeys plus attic, with a ground-floor plan of one of the buildings, linked to the King's Inns by two-storey niched bays. Unsigned and undated, it is probably based on Gandon's drawings for chambers, and on stylistic grounds it would appear to have come from Johnston's office (Fig. 6.3).[4]

On 5 May 1813 the benchers passed a resolution that the lord chancellor be required to:

> ... communicate to Mr Peel[5] the concurrence of the Society of the King's
> Inns, in the measure proposed of converting the unfinished Part of the
> Society's buildings on Constitution Hill, to the purpose of a depository
> for the Public Records upon the Terms and in manner agreed upon
> between the Benchers of the King's Inns and the Commissioners of the
> Public Records.[6]

In the statute of 1814 that granted the site to the government for the use of the Commissioners of Public Records, it is laid down that the unfinished part of the building 'shall be completed and finished pursuant to the Plan, and correspond with the Part which is now finished and called the Dining-hall of the Society of King's Inns'.[7] It stipulates that there should be no building south of the unfinished building, probably because it would constitute a fire hazard. This was challenged in a report of 1822 in which the benchers stated that no written contract was ever entered into by them and the Commissioners, but that there was an 'understanding' that the unfinished building, together with the piece of ground alongside it (for additional records building), should be granted to the Commissioners 'at a rent to be afterwards agreed upon'. (This sizeable piece of land, 100 feet square, can be seen on Johnston's plan of 1813 [see Chapter V, Fig. 5.9].) The benchers also argued that the statute gave a considerable portion of ground to the government without any recompense that would enable them to build chambers, and it prevented them from letting any part of the land to the south of the unfinished library for building purposes. The report recommended that the statute be repealed, and another passed 'conformable to the true intent and meaning of the original arrangement'.[8] The statute passed in 1826 altered and amended the previous one, making it now 'lawful for the said Society of King's

Inns to build upon any Part of Ground to the South of the said Premises', but makes no reference to rent payable to them.[9] Once again the society found itself losing part of its own site to the government without compensation.

The suggestion to convert the proposed library into Offices for Public Records may have come from Francis Johnston who, since 1805, was architect to the Board of Works. He converted the south wing into a Public Records office building which answered Gandon's dining-hall façade, and completed the cupola of the building to Gandon's design. John Semple who worked on the dining-hall wing also worked on the Public Records office, and John Smyth, son of Edward Smyth, provided the sculpture.

Johnston was one of the architects, who included Henry Aaron Baker, to submit plans for a gateway from Henrietta Street into the inns. The idea was mooted on an agenda for a meeting in February 1819 where it was proposed that a

> ... Gate, Sweep Wall, and Frontispiece, entering into the society's Ground, to their Dining Hall, the Registry Office, and other buildings to be built, according to a Plan and Estimate to be approved of by the Society, and that the Expence should be defrayed jointly by Government, and the Society, as it will be the principal Entrance into their said Concerns from Henrietta-Street.[10]

Johnston's plan which included a gate lodge was successful. By August 1820 McCartney & Baker's offer to execute it for £1,123.3s.5d. was approved and building got under way.

The plan (Fig. 6.4) is a variation of the triumphal arch with a major and two minor arched openings, echoing Gandon's central motif on the west front of the building, but Johnston has curved the gateway to facilitate an easy transition from Henrietta Street. It too is executed in granite, on which iron gates are hung. Wooden doors on each side of these gates, set into recessed arches, lead into, respectively, the lodge which is located to the rear of the dining hall, and the laneway behind the Public Records office, beside what is now the library of the King's Inns in Henrietta Street.

As Gandon complemented and safeguarded the integrity of Pearce's building at the Parliament House, Johnston nods to Gandon in the general layout of his design and in his use of motifs such as the recessed arches. He too uses rusticated and

Fig. 6.4   *Elevation and plan by Johnston showing the gateway to the King's Inns from Henrietta Street, with a lodge to the right. (Private collection)*

smooth ashlar but his design is a simplified version with no vaulting within the gateway save the middle arch which has a plain barrel vault while the areas under the small arches are flat. The gateway is surmounted by a most impressive sculpture by John Smyth in Portland stone of the royal arms of the United Kingdom with a lion and a unicorn.[11] Gas lamps were placed on the entrance gate and in the interior court in 1825. The whole arrangement, with its curved screen wall linking the building to Henrietta Street, terminates the vista up that street.

As has been seen, the provision of chambers for the society was a recurring problem and was used repeatedly as a bargaining tool whenever the benchers appealed for compensation from the government for loss of their premises. Since 1794 the society was in receipt of deposits for chambers from new barristers and attorneys 'to be allowed when the gentleman shall purchase from the society chambers or ground to build chambers on'.[12] According to Maurice Craig, in the years following the Union there were more than 650 barristers and almost 1,500 attorneys resident in Dublin.[13] Given such large numbers, it is clear that the society failed to provide for the accommodation needs of its members. The committee appointed by the benchers to look into the affairs of the society admitted in their report of 1808 that the money had been expended on ground rent, on the temporary hall and the dining-hall wing. But money was also being spent in 1825 on the new library for the society on Henrietta Street, at which we will look later, and the law library and other accommodation at the Four Courts, where tipstaffs and other attendants were being paid by the society. This prompted the attorneys and solicitors to apply to the benchers requesting 'the accommodation of a Chamber in [the Four Courts] for the members of their profession and which they claim with greater confidence having contributed the greater part of the funds of the society'.[14] The benchers, looking at the large proportion of their site at Henrietta Street that was lying waste reacted quickly. A standing committee met on 14 February 1826 at which it was agreed unanimously that 'it would be manifestly just, and highly expedient for the interests of the Society, to erect Two Buildings, consisting of Six sets of Chambers each, as delineated in the Plan annexed, as a commencement of a general plan of building chambers'.[15] One building would be for the Bar members of the society and the other for the attorney members of the society. They proposed that other sites would be let to

> ... persons disposed to invest their capitals in continuing similar buildings, to be erected and built according to these two model buildings, so as to render the line of these buildings, which would have the newly projected line of a new street in front of them, similar and uniform.

The plans were drawn up by Frederick Darley, who was responsible for the building of the library of the King's Inns on Henrietta Street from 1825, and the estimate supplied by contractors McCartney & Ballentine.[16] In December 1826 it was decided that advertisements should be published in newspapers for proposals for building chambers according to the plans and specifications that were held in the treasurer's office.

The 'new street' referred to above was to facilitate ease of access between the King's Inns and the Four Courts (Fig. 6.5). Located on the society's land, the street would be accessed through a gateway at the top of Henrietta Street between the

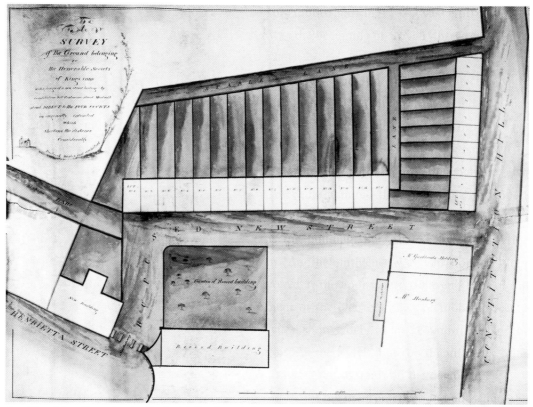

Fig. 6.5 *Drawing by Frederick Darley of the proposed new street of chambers linking Henrietta Street with Constitution Hill.*

library and the Public Records office, running south towards the Linen Hall, and, with the Public Records offices' square plot on its immediate right, turn west to Constitution Hill, covering part of the area now occupied by the car park.[17] Along this street would be built the proposed chambers, the gardens of which would extend to the boundary with the Linen Hall along the side of which the cottages now stand. The plan, of course, could only be brought into effect by the amended statute of 1826 that allowed the society to build south of the Public Records office. However, local residents and traders objected to the plan and no such street was opened.[18]

Chambers were never built either at the Four Courts or at the King's Inns. Among a number of reasons given were that the King's Inns was too far away from the Four Courts for the lawyers' convenience; and even that life in chambers might be morally unhealthy for young lawyers. An Irish bencher, Acheson Lyle, suggested

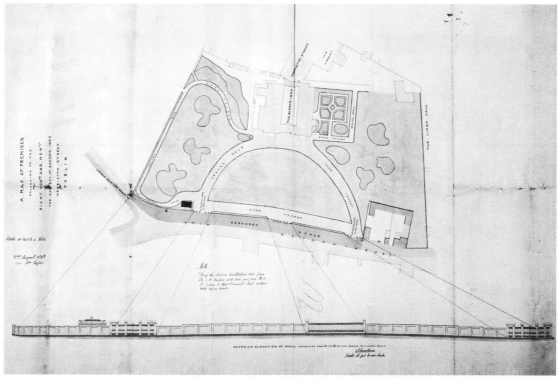

🟐 **Fig. 6.6** *William Tassie's map of 1842 shows the wall, railings and gates to be erected along Constitution Hill. An L-shaped block plan of the five cottages can be seen at the top right.*

in 1846 that it might give young men the possibility 'of contracting habits leading to immorality and licentiousness' and that the chamber system in England led to habits that would not be desirable to have introduced to Ireland. This may have been, as Kenny says, the last straw in tipping the scales against proceeding with chambers at the King's Inns.[19]

By the end of June 1833, the society was in possession of Richard Wilson's plot of land along Constitution Hill. With only a few houses left occupied there, some by staff of the society, Jacob Owen, now architect to the Board of Works[20] was, in 1836, directed to level the ground in front of the King's Inns, across what was formerly Wilson's plot to where the wall and railings are at present. The following year Owen was directed to demolish the staff quarters on Constitution Hill and to build five houses for staff accommodation, 'the entire expence not to exceed the sum of £750'. An entrance gateway was to be provided to the north of the site at Constitution Hill, and a lodge, the cost of which was to be no more than £200,

🏵 *Fig. 6.7*   *Photograph dating to* c. *1890–1910 of the King's Inns showing the parapet and chimney of the lodge (dem.) above the wall at the centre. (Reproduced by permission of the Royal Society of Antiquaries of Ireland)*

was to be erected at the gate (Figs 6.6 and 6.7).[21] In June 1845 the building committee approved Owen's plans for a second lodge beside a gateway to be built on Constitution Hill.[22] That lodge is still *in situ* to the south of the grounds.

Both were there in 1930 when a report on all of the cottages was carried out. At that point there were nine cottages in the grounds: two on Constitution Hill; one, known as the Gate Lodge, beside the gate at Henrietta Street, which is still there; the five cottages forming an L-shaped block to the south of the Registry of Deeds and behind the library, and one other which was apparently situated to the north of the Gate Lodge by the wall of the 'Penitentiary', as Luke Gardiner's former home was then known.[23] From the time they were built the cottages accommodated staff such as gatekeepers, gardeners, porters, butlers, waiters and library attendants, together with their families in many cases.[24]

By the 1840s the society was in need of more accommodation in their dining-hall wing. A plan for a new room 'and other improvements' was submitted by Frederick Darley and was approved by the building committee in May 1846. The job was described variously as one for 'improving the staircase at King's Inns and cutting off the offensive effluence from the kitchen' and 'an alteration and an addition to, by improving the Staircase and giving further accommodation in rooms for the assemblage of barristers and attorneys and some further offices in the basement'.[25] An agreement was drawn up between the society and William Moyers, contractor, of Richmond Street, Dublin, in July, and work started on the project immediately. The price agreed was £2,554.17s.1d. From such an innocuous beginning developed the large-scale northern three-bay extension to the King's Inns

✦ *Figs 6.8–10*
Plans by Darley & Montgomery for the new single-storey extension to Gandon's building.

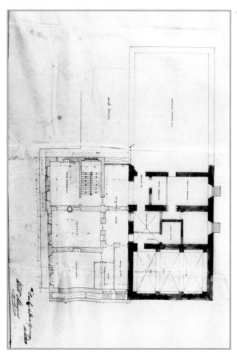

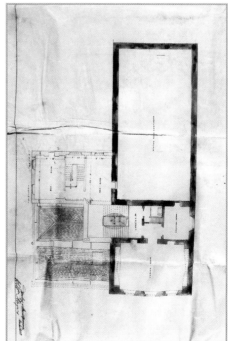

✦ *Fig 6.8*
Basement.

✦ *Fig 6.9*
First-floor.

in 1846, followed by a similar extension to the Registry of Deeds in 1849. The first, for the King's Inns, was designed by Frederick Darley and the second, for the Public Records office, by Jacob Owen. These extensions to the north and south would seriously upset the equilibrium of Gandon's building.

In plans that have recently come to light at the King's Inns, Darley's extension was to consist of one storey over a basement.[26] These plans give us an idea of what was originally intended, but much of it was not executed due to a change of plan when the building was partly erected (Figs 6.8–6.10). The basement area (Fig. 6.8) containing a pantry, laundry, caterer's room, servants' dressing room, knife room, plate room, cellars and proposed scullery, and a back staircase, is similar to the present arrangement. The ground floor of the extension is accessed through the

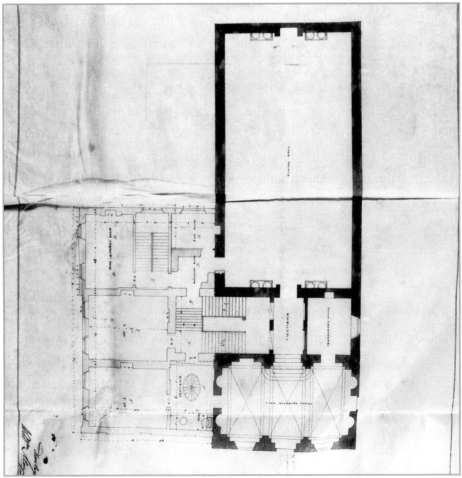

Fig 6.10 Ground floor.

doorway in the north of the entrance hall, leading into a top-lit vestibule, across from which were the present barristers' room and lecture room (Fig. 6.10). A short staircase (to the level of the dining hall) led to a room for the wine butler and to an anteroom with a new mahogany door leading into the dining hall itself. But the main incursion into Gandon's building was caused by a new staircase which, according to the plan, was to be similar to Gandon's, but which seemed to necessitate demolishing part of the north wall to enable it to be set further back. However, what was built is an imperial staircase in place of the stair with half-turns and landings. This staircase meant that the two arches to the left as one mounted the steps from the entrance hall leading to the dining hall were no longer suitable, so Darley replaced them with two Doric columns between which the staircase is approached. From this plan we can see that the flight of steps leading from the entrance hall to the dining hall was not built according to Gandon's design (where it began at the wall and ended between the two arches) but flowed into the vestibule in a curved arrangement.[27]

The specifications for the plans lay down that the façade of the building (to be built of granite from the Ballyknockan quarry) was to correspond in every respect with that of the ground floor of Gandon's building. In a photograph taken at about this time, it is possible to make out the partly demolished wall of Gandon's building, and what was probably a pilaster on the return of the original building (Fig. 6.11). Darley's extension, slightly stepped back, bringing it into line with the central triple arch, would reach as far as the cornice above the first storey on the front, and would be one storey higher to the rear. On 11 September 1846, the benchers, having inspected the building in progress, asked the architect to furnish them with plans and an estimate for adding another storey to give them extra space. The revised plan for the extension as we see it now has not yet been found.

It was perhaps at this stage that the benchers' room was renovated and the ceiling replaced. Originally this room had *oeil-de-boeuf* windows at each end of its coved ceiling; one towards the central bridge element, the other then perhaps blocked off by the new building.[28] When compared to Gandon's plan, the current cove is more elliptical and would probably not allow such an opening. The decoration in the benchers' room and in the stairwell is not in accordance with Gandon's more architectonic taste.

Fig. 6.11 *An early photograph taken by the Revd Calvert Richard Jones (1804–77), probably towards the end of 1846, shows work in progress on the extension. (Reproduced by permission of the National Museum of Photography Film and Television/Science & Society Picture Library)*

In February 1848 the Board of Works advised the King's Inns that they proposed 'to add to the front of the building in a similar manner as the Benchers have lately done to their wing'.[29] In November 1849 the board accepted the proposal from Messrs James Forrest of Camden Street to erect the new buildings for the sum of £3,789 and the building got under way to Jacob Owen's design. The plan shows that a large, plain wing was to be built behind the board's new extension to the Registry of Deeds 'for a strong room on three floors and in basement, toilets, carpenters shop and book binders', of fireproof construction for the purpose of storing records.[30]

In his book on Gandon, Hugo Duffy believes that the added wings 'destroyed the force of [Gandon's] design, diminishing the thrust of his original building, and the added mass constricts his central feature so that the cupola appears to have been added to strengthen a central weakness'.[31] In a review of Mulvany and Gandon's *Life of Gandon* in June 1847 reference is made to the first (benchers') wing by an anonymous author (generally assumed to be Samuel Ferguson), who made the point that the extension would spoil the symmetry of Gandon's building and suggested that the benchers should pull it down and 'set it back ten or fifteen feet, so as not to interfere with the original building'.[32] The government's wing balanced things somewhat, but one must agree with Ferguson that setting the wings back would have helped to preserve the integrity of Gandon's building (Fig. 6.12). Indeed, if Darley's original one-storey over-basement plan for the extension had been executed that integrity would have been maintained.

Fig. 6.12 *In late 1849 the Board of Works extended their premises, the Registry of Deeds, to the right of Gandon's building, replicating Darley's design for their façade.*

By about 1850 Gandon's building was quite changed; the council chamber, or benchers' room, had a different ceiling without the *oeil-de-boeuf* windows and with much more (it can be assumed) stucco decoration; the entrance hall is probably essentially as it was except for the arrangement of the flight of steps to the dining hall; the main staircase and the passage to the dining hall are quite changed but, thankfully, the dining hall, in its near-perfect state of preservation, remains the most important Gandon public interior to have survived in Dublin. The only changes to be seen in the dining hall from Gandon's design are the two doors to the left as one enters; one was inserted when Darley extended the building, and the other is a twentieth-century addition for ease of access from a new kitchen.

---

[1] Building accounts 1800–1807 (KI MS H2/1–3) p 80.

[2] Colm Kenny discusses the motto of the society in *King's Inns*, pp 243–4.

[3] Building accounts 1800–1807, ff 75, 80.

[4] Private collection. Elevation and plan of the King's Inns and square of chambers, with ground-floor plan. In this collection too, is a drawing of the King's Inns with a seven-bay extension to each side that is inscribed 'Sketch for completing the front of the Kings Inns and Offices for Records Dublin'.

[5] Robert Peel, Chief Secretary, 1812–18.

[6] KI Benchers' Minutes 1804–19, f 75. This wing, originally to be the library for the society, became the Public Records office, with accommodation for the Prerogative and Consistorial Courts and from *c.* 1826 it also housed the Registry of Deeds.

[7] *54 George III*, c.113.

[8] KI Benchers' Minutes 1804–19, f 130v.

[9] *7 George IV*, c.13.

[10] Notes, agenda, notices of meetings (KI MS B1/6–2). There are no minutes recorded of such a meeting.

[11] Invoice from Smyth, amount of which is £160 (KI MS H2/1–6).

[12] Kenny, C., 'King's Inns and Henrietta Street Chambers', *Dublin Historical Record*, Vol. XLVII, No. 2 (Autumn 1994) pp 155–68.

[13] Craig, M., *Dublin 1660–1860* (Dublin 1969) p 274.

[14] Solicitors' memorial for a chamber at the Four Courts (KI MS H1/5).

[15] Report of the Standing Committee, Specially Summoned, 14 February 1826 (KI MS B2/3–3).

[16] The plans of the proposed chambers by F. Darley (KI Map drawer H4) date to 1827. The delay between the meeting of February 1826 and the execution of the plans was due to having the statute of 1814 amended, and the newspaper advertisement for building proposals in December. These coloured drawings were probably for presentation purposes.

[17] *A Survey of the Ground Belonging to the King's Inns, with a Design of a New Street Leading from Henrietta St. to the Four Courts* (KI Map drawer H4/1); *Design of the New Gateway Proposed to be Erected at the Entrance of the New Street Leading from Henrietta St. to the Four Courts* (KI Map drawer H4/3). Both plans by Frederick Darley, jnr.

[18] Griffin, C., 'Post Gandon at the Four Courts', in Costello, C. (ed.) *The Four Courts: 200 Years* (Dublin 1996) p 242.

[19] *Select Committee on Legal Education … 1846*, H.C. 1846 (686), x, 1, qq 2234–40, quoted in Kenny, C., *Tristram Kennedy and The Revival of Irish Legal Training 1835–1885* (Dublin 1996) p 225.

[20] Owen was employed as architect to the society from 1835.

[21] KI Benchers' Minutes, Building committee meeting, 1835–44, p 66.

[22] A payment was made to Richard Turner on 10 June 1839 for iron gates at Constitution Hill for *c.* £165 'being second new entrance from Constitution Hill'. These gates, possibly erected in that year, were relocated in 1845; Building committee meetings 9/18 June 1845, 1844–49 (KI MS B2/1–1).

[23] In the mid-nineteenth century an asylum for discharged female prisoners was established at 10 Henrietta Street, run by the Daughters of Charity 'to help Roman Catholic discharged prisoners who are just *commencing* a life of crime, to leave their evil ways'. Prunty, J., *Dublin Slums 1800–1925* (Dublin 1998) p 270.

[24] Report on cottages made by John Robinson, 21 November 1930 (KI MS H2/3/ 1930–33).

[25] Building Committee meeting, 21 May 1846 (KI MS B2/1–1) pp 18–19.

[26] KI MS G2/6–5. The extension was two storey at the rear.

[27] It is not clear when these steps lost their curves to the present pedestal arrangements.

[28] Charles Thorp, plasterer, in his account for stucco work in the Council Chamber in *c.* 1805, mentions 'circular stucco plastering around elliptical fan lights at ends of ceiling and on circular soffits under cornice at ends of room' (KI MS H2/1–3) p 101.

[29] National Archives, Board of Works, 2D/57/42. Letter to under-treasurer Conway E. Dobbs, 10 February 1848.

[30] National Archives, OPW 5 HC/1/107. Jacob Owen's addition to King's Inns of 1849.

[31] Duffy, H., pp 242–6.

[32] 'Architecture in Ireland', *Dublin University Magazine*, Vol. XXIX, 1847, p 707; O'Dwyer, F., 'Public works architecture in Ireland 1829–1923, Vol. I', Ph.D thesis (Trinity College Dublin 1995) p 97.

THE LIBRARY

In January 1788 Charles O'Neill, one of the benchers, recommended that a number of books from the library belonging to the late Mr Justice Christopher Robinson, which were valued at the time at £700, should be bought by the society. Approval was given 'so soon as a library or proper room can be provided'.[1] This collection became the nucleus of the present library of the society, now housed in its own building in Henrietta Street. In that year the society had no home for them. In the meantime they were stored in double-locked deed boxes in the basement of the Four Courts, with one key in the possession of the treasurer of the society and the other in that of the lord chief justice. In the plan of 1790 (see Chapter 2, Fig 2.5) a library was part of the accommodation proposed behind the Four Courts, and it continued to form part of the society's building aspirations from then on.

There was a library in the Townsend Street premises and Robinson's books moved there with the society in 1792. By the time the temporary building was erected on Constitution Hill in 1798 it must be assumed that the society was in possession of a fair-sized collection of books, as part of that accommodation was a library. The number of books was greatly increased in 1801 as a result of an amendment to the Copyright Act of 1710, which required that publishers give (without charge) a copy of each book published to various libraries in England and Scotland (mostly universities). The amendment provided that the libraries of Trinity College, Dublin and of the King's Inns would benefit in like manner. In 1836 this Act was repealed in respect of a number of libraries including the King's Inns.

When Gandon's dining-hall wing was finally completed in 1806, the books and papers belonging to the society were placed in the benchers' room and the adjoining room which were used as a library until the new purpose-built library was ready for occupation in 1832. In an agenda of February 1819 it was proposed that a committee be appointed to consider 'the present State of the occasional library' and at meetings over the next number of years the inadequacy of the accommodation is stressed. Large parcels of books were heaped on the floor making it impossible for the librarians to catalogue without more space. The benchers were urged to decide upon a plan for a building suitable to their needs. In February 1823 they acquired the Prerogative office, formerly the lord primate's house at the top of Henrietta Street. By July 1824 plans and specifications by Frederick Darley had been agreed and the under-treasurer was directed to advertise for tenders. In September 1825 the proposals received from contractors Edward Carolin & Sons were accepted at £6,013.2s.7d.[2]

It seems curious that the society, with so much space available on their site, chose to build on Henrietta Street and then rather than converting the building, they demolished it and built another in its place. Littledale says that the site was chosen because an eminent judge and bencher who lived opposite was upset by a proposal that it should be converted into a mendicity institution ('such conversion would have been exceedingly unpleasant') but it is more probable that the benchers wanted to keep their site free for chambers which would provide an income for them.[3]

The site on which Henrietta Street now stands and a portion of the site on which Gandon's King's Inns stands was originally the private garden of the abbots of the Cistercian Abbey of St Mary, and was part of their land. Containing about seven acres, it is described in old records as the 'Anchorite's garden' or 'Ancaster's Park'.[4] A portion of the park eventually came into the possession of Sir Richard Reynell, afterwards chief justice of the King's Bench in Ireland.[5] Sir John Temple, master of the rolls (whose descendant, Henry Temple, was created Viscount Palmerston in 1722) acquired the remaining portion. Reynell's son, Sir Thomas Reynell, sold the park in 1721 to Luke Gardiner for the sum of £850.[6] Gardiner developed the site during the 1730s and 1740s.

Luke Gardiner (d. 1755) was a self-made man, who is said to have started out as a footman for Mr White at Leixlip Castle (Fig. 7.1).[7] He became a property developer and a banker with an office in Castle Street, Dublin. In 1711 he married Anne, daughter of The Hon. Alexander, second son of William, 1st Viscount Mountjoy, thus attaching himself to the aristocracy.[8] Apart from being a member of parliament, Gardiner became deputy vice-treasurer and receiver-general, and later surveyor general of the customs. These positions enabled him to amass a fortune, much of which was invested in property development. He became ranger of the Castleknock Walk in the Phoenix Park and built a private house there which is now the headquarters of the Ordnance Survey Office. Most of the land he acquired was on the north side of the city where developers and speculators vied with each other in

Fig. 7.1
Portrait of Luke Gardiner, MP (d. 1755) Deputy Vice-Treasurer of Ireland, who developed Henrietta Street, by Charles Jervas (c. 1675–1739)/John Brooks. Mezzotint. (Photograph courtesy of the National Gallery of Ireland)

the building fever that took place there in the early part of the eighteenth century. Luke Gardiner was the most important of these and he proceeded to lay out his lands 'on a truly magnificent scale'.[9]

When naming his streets, Gardiner sometimes took the opportunity to flatter one or two lords lieutenant. Henrietta Street is named after the wife of the duke of Bolton,[10] and Sackville Street (now O'Connell Street) after Lionel Sackville, duke of Dorset. He also christened two of his children Henrietta and Sackville. The first and the grandest of the streets to be laid out by Gardiner, Henrietta Street, is a broad street, leading west from Bolton Street on rising ground to the Plover Field. In 1724 the archbishop of Armagh, Primate Hugh Boulter, signed articles of agreement to purchase a site on which 'three new houses lately built but remaining unfinished' stood, on the street 'called or intended to be called Henrietta-street'.[11] However, the property, on the site of the present King's Inns library, was not conveyed to him until 1730.[12] As the Dublin residence of the primate up to 1794, the street became known as 'Primate's Hill'.[13] His mansion, with a frontage of almost ninety feet, can be seen clearly on John Rocque's Map of 1756 (see Chapter III, Fig. 3.1). There is an interesting item in Boulter's agreement that

> Luke Gardiner … shall not build or suffer to be built by any other person any other House in the said street … to be made use of for selling of Ale or other Liquor or for any Shopkeeper Chandler Brewer or Artificer and that the said street shall be made at least Fifty foot wide from the Railes to be set before the Houses on one side of the said street to the Railes before the Houses on the other side thereof …[14]

Boulter lived in the house until his death in 1742. He was a passionate upholder of English interest in Ireland, promptly filling every vacant see in the Church and every position on the judicial bench (in his capacity as one of the lords justice) with Englishmen. He was succeeded by Primate John Hoadly who leased the house from Boulter's representatives and who died four years later. The bishop of Kildare, George Stone, who had been living at 5 Henrietta Street, succeeded to the primacy in 1746. He took a 999-year lease on the house.[15] Primates Boulter and Stone, as lords justices, wielded an extraordinary amount of power and, with Speakers Boyle and Ponsonby, they virtually ruled the country from their bases in Henrietta Street. Lavish dinner parties were a regular event at Primate Stone's splendid house, continuing into the early hours, at which affairs of state were discussed and settled, and the policy of the government was shaped.

Stone died in 1764 and was succeeded by Richard Robinson, bishop of Kildare, who was created Lord Rokeby in 1777. He purchased the mansion in 1765 on his appointment. After he died near Bristol in 1794 his body lay in state in Henrietta Street before being brought to Armagh Cathedral where he was interred. Robinson left the house to his nephew and executor, the Revd Sir John Robinson, who was registrar of the Prerogative Court, and it was used for some time as offices for that court. The house is described in *The Irish Builder* series as 'a large brick building, having a frontage to Henrietta-street of about 90 ft, and 270 ft from front to rere'.[16]

From the articles of agreement between the society and Messrs Carolin, the contractors, it appears that the primate's house had been divided into two, as the library was to be built 'on ground where two old houses (formerly occupied by and used as the Prerogative Office) then stood'.[17] No details of this building have come to light apart from *The Irish Builder*'s description of it (above). At first, Darley intended retaining the façade of the existing building, but upon examination, he 'found it would be hazardous to depend upon the old wall', and abandoned the idea. The old building was probably three to four storeys over basement, brick built, with Portland stone architraves around the windows of the piano nobile and the upper storey, and a string course perhaps below the piano nobile. The building was originally to be finished by 25 March 1827, but that was extended to 20 January 1828. In fact, the library was ready for readers only in 1832. A story is told about a discovery during the demolition of the primate's house. According to the *Irish Georgian Society's Records* workmen found a cup with 124 guineas and half-guineas in a chest inside a bricked-up cellar.[18]

None of Darley's drawings for the library have been found, with the exception of a damaged longitudinal section of the front of the library showing the gallery, executed in watercolour, by Darley (Fig. 7.2). The library is designed in the Greek Revival style which became fashionable in England in the second half of the eighteenth century. The revival of the stark simplicity of Greek architecture did not last much beyond the late 1830s simply because there was only so much that could be achieved using its vocabulary. In Francis Johnston's Townley Hall, Co. Louth (1794), a note of Greek severity was struck in the exterior where the heavy Doric columns of the portico emphasise the dearth of decoration on the building. The Courthouse in Dundalk, begun in 1813 and designed by Edward Park and John Bowden, is Greek Revival at its best – stark, simple, well proportioned and ultimately satisfying to the eye.

Frederick Darley's design for the library of the King's Inns has three storeys over a basement and was originally seven bays wide (Fig. 7.3). An annex, one bay wide, was added to the western end of the library at the end of the nineteenth century. The centre three bays project forward only slightly and are crowned by a pediment on each side of which a balustrade extends across the line of the roof and returns on the west side. According to the specifications, the balusters were to be made of metal, an early use of such a material. The ground floor is rusticated on each side of the central projection. Round-headed niches and pilasters flank the portico which comprises four Greek Doric columns carrying a Doric entablature, which extends across the central projection, and a small plain pediment. This was the first Greek Doric portico erected in Dublin. The only decorations on the building are two medallions with husk chains, one on each side of the entrance doorway. The building has often been criticised for its soul-less character. Sir Samuel Ferguson, who has been mentioned before in connection with the benchers' extension to Gandon's building, writes of the library in the same article in 1847 that the benchers have

> ... not been fortunate in their selection of the new design. ... [it] is a clumsy house, and the meagre proportions of its other members contrast very unhappily with the forced heaviness of its low portico, another example of the error so prevalent of late years, that the weighty features of Greek Doric architecture can be applied, with propriety, to the light windowed facades of modern houses.[19]

It is difficult not to have sympathy with Ferguson's view. The library is built exclusively of granite with no Portland stone trimmings to relieve it. The forbidding nature of its façade is emphasised by the railings (erected later) which closely surround the portico. Maurice Craig calls it 'bleak and uninspired'.[20] On the plus side *The Dublin Penny Journal* of 1835–6 remarked that the building 'reflects great credit on the correct taste of the architect, Mr Darley',[21] while *The Irish Builder and Engineer* of 1915 was a trifle more circumspect, describing it as 'of no outstanding merit, but is quiet and dignified'.[22] Neither is it too obtrusive on Henrietta Street despite the fact that the houses are mostly of brick: its façade is level with the other houses and it is not markedly higher. Gandon's building, Johnston's gateway, and the gateway leading into the cottages, are all constructed of granite so that the library does not look out of place. Its main fault lies with its entrance, the portico of which lacks any semblance of grandeur: it is low, dark, claustrophobic and lacks generosity in its narrow doorway. One cannot help but wonder if Darley's original plan to retain the façade of the old building, rendering it with Roman cement in imitation of granite, and reapplying the Portland stone architraves and string course, would have been more agreeable than what was subsequently built.

Fig. 7.4   *View from the hall through the octagonal vestibule to the staircase and the armorial window on the landing.*

Happily, the interior of the building, in particular the reading room, is another story. The *Dublin Penny Journal* judged it 'tastefully and commodiously fitted up'.[23] On entering through the portico, the eye is drawn across the rectangular hall and through the broad arches of the octagonal vestibule to the staircase, at the top of which is a large stained-glass window (Fig. 7.4). The floor throughout this area is covered with Yorkshire flagging. According to the bill of quantities it was originally planned to have mahogany doors hung between the front hall and the vestibule, and Greek Ionic columns, half-columns and quarter-columns placed in the vestibule and in the front parlour.[24]

From the hall one is led into the four main rooms of the ground floor: to the left is a room which is at present used as the office of the dean of the law school, behind that is the office of the under-treasurer of the society.[25] To the right of the hall is a passageway leading to the general office at the front of the building, a further office and a small kitchen, to the rear.[26] Marble chimneypieces were provided for these four ground-floor rooms in the specifications. Three are *in situ*, the fourth (director of education's office) was either never put in place, or was removed. These four rooms are called 'librarians apartments' in the specifications. In June 1830, the librarian was granted apartments on the 'hall floor of the building and offices underneath [part of the basement]'.[27] By 1851 the location of the librarian's accommodation was more specific: 'the two rooms and Dressingroom [the present kitchen] on the ground floor to the right of the entrance Hall, and the Kitchen and Servants room adjoining the Larder and Pantry in the Basement Story, together with the Stable and Coachhouse'.[28] In 1865 the society purchased number 11 Henrietta Street, the house next to the library, and three years later the occupants were listed in *Thom's Directories* as barristers J.D. O'Hanlon and J.M. la Barte, respectively under-treasurer and librarian of the King's Inns. These two office-holders of the society resided continuously in that house up to 1984 in the case of the librarian and 1990 in the case of the under-treasurer.[29] A lovely story in the *Irish Times* in 1896 gives the reason why the librarian was moved into the house next to the library:

> … for finding that Henry Monck Mason, their former librarian, about
> forty years ago, then dwelling in the library, had some very fine girls for
> daughters, they thought their beauty troubled the studies of the young
> barristers, and for the future (after his demise) they required the

librarian to dwell in the adjacent house, taken by them for that purpose.[30]

The main staircase, built on the imperial plan with a central flight and double return (similar to his staircase in the main building) is impressive. The stairs are of granite with wrought-iron balusters, and a mahogany handrail.[31] The staircase leads to the aforementioned stained-glass window on the landing of which the *Dublin Penny Journal* observed 'the painted window of singular beauty, being divided into thirty-nine divisions, containing the arms of the judges and benchers of the King's Inns'.[32] The sum of three guineas was paid by each bencher whose arms appear therein. Made by M. O'Connor of Dame Street in Dublin, the large window is round-topped and generously sized, with the twenty-four coats of arms placed in a central panel, and a border of yellow and white glass around it.[33] At the top is the coat of arms of the society with their motto *Nolumus Mutari*, under which are the arms of H.M. Mason and H. Sandes, respectively librarian and under-treasurer.

The reading room is a superb example of a Greek Revival interior (Fig. 7.5). It spans the entire length (excepting the annex behind the most westerly bay) and depth of the building, and is of double height. It is lit from the seven windows of each storey at the front – all north facing, and by eight windows facing south. A gallery at second-floor level is bounded by a cast-iron balustrade executed in black and gold with Greek motifs. The gallery is supported by the bookshelves which project at right-angles from the walls of the building between the windows on each side and by a pair of free-standing fluted Ionic columns with bases at each end of the library. The gable ends of the bookshelves are in the form of stepped pilasters, none of which has an Ionic capital but decorated instead with a frieze of palmettes which runs below a cornice, the details of which are picked out in gold. Darley's watercolour (see Fig. 7.2) indicates that his plan was to duplicate the arrangement of the bookshelves at gallery level, but unfortunately this was not carried out. It is also interesting to note his suggested colour scheme for the library. The room bears a marked resemblance to the library of The London Institution by William Brooks (1815–19; dem. 1936) and to Thomas Burgh's Old Library in Trinity College Dublin (begun 1712) as it was before Deane and Woodward's 1860 additions. While the Old Library's ceiling was flat and compartmentalised, that of the King's

Inns is plain, apart from its cornice, but has as a centrepiece a large stylised anthemion and palmette motif in stucco. As the bill of quantities refers to 'enriching and panelling' on the library ceiling, the original idea was probably to have it compartmentalised.

Little information is available about the building of the library, and not much can be gleaned from the accounts: J&R Mallet submitted an invoice in May/June 1828 for £87.17s.6d., which set out in great detail a description of the railings they supplied and fitted across the front of the building, but whether they supplied the Greek-inspired balustrade in the gallery is not recorded.[34] Terence Farrell was paid £4.16s.0d. in May 1828 for 'carving work to Portico'. In 1832 William Carey was paid for desks, ladders and blinds, Williams and Gibton for chairs and J&R Mallet for the tables.[35]

Other items in both minutes and accounts raise questions rather than answer them. It appears that in February 1828 Darley submitted a plan 'for the fitting up of the interior of the new library'.[36] A number of estimates were received and, the following July, Carolin's proposals for the job were accepted.[37] At the same meeting in July, the final payment of £1,828.17s.3d. due to Carolin was made as per the original schedule of payments of 1825. It is not at all clear what the 'fitting up of the interior of the new library' means. Carolin received three more payments for work done in the library between Michaelmas term 1828 and Hilary term 1830 which included 'fitting up Book Room in Library'.

It is interesting to note that nowhere in the bill of quantities for the library is the gallery mentioned, nor a staircase giving access to the gallery.[38] Neither is there any mention of shelving. So it would appear that Darley probably meant from the outset to treat the fitting-up of the library as a separate item. But it seems very odd that he would wait until February 1828, almost two-and-a-half years after the articles of agreement for the building of the library were signed, before submitting his plans for these vital components. We can only assume, therefore, that his plans of 1828 now included the gallery and the 'Book Room',[39] and, presumably, a staircase that gave access to both. There is no indication within or without the building of a second staircase: however, a library committee report of 1844 confirms that there was one, but it had its problems:

> ... the Gallery of the Library contains books as well as the room below
>
> and it is necessary for persons frequenting the Library ... to have access

to the Gallery but the stairs which at present lead up to the Gallery do
not communicate with the interior of the Library below but are carried
up from a place outside the Library altogether. We think it would be an
improvement if an alteration in this respect could be made by having a
Stair case leading to the Gallery carried up directly from the interior of
the Library below without impairing in any degree the present
convenient and beautiful arrangement of [its] interior ...[40]

The staircase can be seen on the Ordnance Survey map of 1838. However, a
hand-drawn and undated plan by William Maguire, architect to the society from
the early 1950s (Fig. 7.6) shows that the staircase began at first floor or reading
room level. Below this on the ground floor was a lobby, a water closet and a door

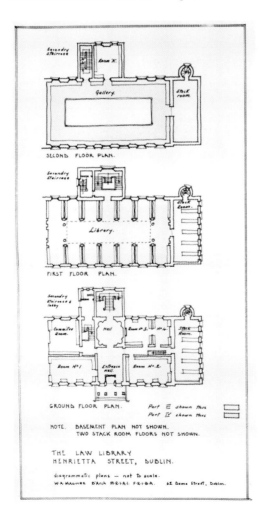

    Fig. 7.6 *William Maguire's plan of the
library shows the staircase
(dem.) to the rear of the
building that gave access to
the gallery of the reading
room. Also here on the
ground floor can be seen the
narrow staircase leading to
the basement.*

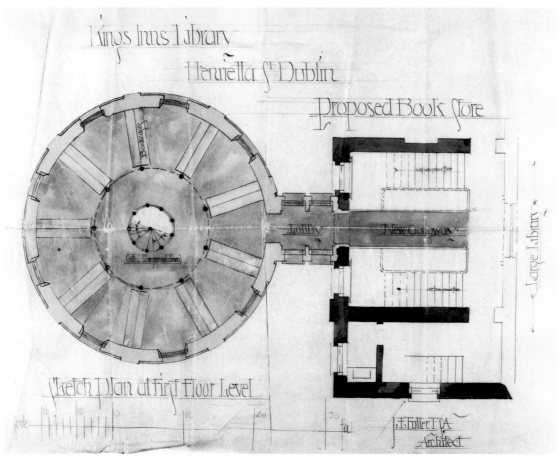

Figs 7.7 and 7.8 (opposite page)
Plan and section of an unexecuted proposal for an extension to the library by James Franklin
Fuller c. 1890.

leading into the garden.[41] The staircase was accessed through (what is now) the dummy door to the left of the landing as one leaves the reading room, where two short flights of stairs led to a door at gallery level.

The proposition that the gallery and staircase were afterthoughts can be borne out by the building itself. To the rear of the building the stained-glass window is located in the centre of the return. The second staircase alongside this stopped just short of one of the windows of the library's reading room, thereby disturbing the symmetry of the rear of the building, something an architect would try to avoid from the beginning. According to Maguire the staircase was removed because it

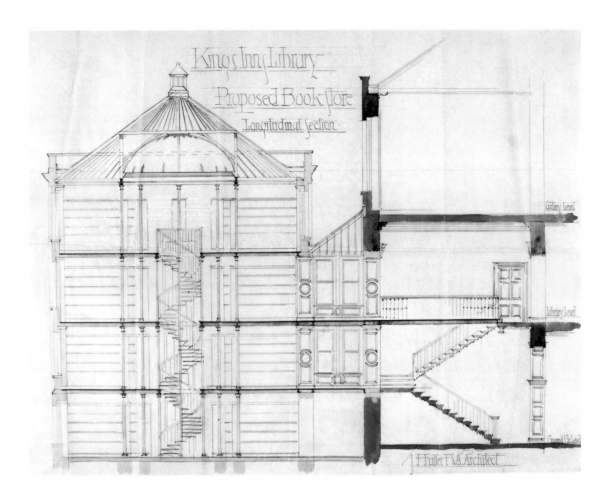

was derelict, and it is evident from minute books that problems with the sanitary conditions in this part of the return were ongoing.[42] He recommended its removal. In November 1962 the benchers authorised Maguire to demolish the entire annex and to provide toilet facilities in the basement instead.[43] As a result, the rear wall of the library was re-plastered and sills replaced.

Robert Ballentine's account for stone-cutting for January 1831 mentions 'cutting holes in flagging for sleepers of new stairs going to basement storey'.[44] This must refer to the present stairs outside the under-treasurer's office, but no reason is given why they were built at this later stage. Perhaps it was because the original staircase to the basement was an extremely narrow one (and possibly unsafe?) from the corridor outside the present general office (see Fig. 7.6), and was removed in the late 1950s.

The gallery was in place in November 1830 when the library committee ordered the architect to proceed with the shelves there. In 1831 George Patterson was paid for carpentry, and Sibthorpe & Peacock were paid £469.16s.5d. for painting. In November the librarian was told to proceed 'with moving and classing of books', to provide fires for the public apartments and to arrange for a catalogue to be printed when the books are in place for the use of the profession.[45]

Now that the books were being moved out of Gandon's building, the society considered fitting up and furnishing the old library as an apartment for the benchers and, accordingly in June 1832 they directed that

> ... the Bookcases and Presses be given to Mr Carolin at the price formerly agreed upon: that the Parliamentary Chamber [old library, now benchers' room] be painted and a Bronze Lamp provided, a door placed at the entrance of the passage to the Parliamentary Chamber and suitable furniture provided.[46]

By May 1844 the library committee was not at all happy with the access staircase to the gallery being located outside the library itself, as already mentioned above. Nothing was done about it until the 1880s when James Franklin Fuller (1835–1924) was appointed architect to the society and in mid-1886 was asked to look at the building's stability with a view to alterations.[47] The problem was exacerbated in November of that year with the arrival of about 120 volumes of American law reports and nowhere to put them. Extra shelving was proposed in the basement, but this could only be a temporary measure because of damp air and inaccessibility. Four-and-a-half years later presses and shelves had been erected in every available spot, and books had to be packed rather than shelved, the end result being damage to the books themselves. Finally, it was decided that an extension would be built to the west side of the library. Plans received from Fuller were approved, the estimate not to exceed £2,000, and the addition would be capable of storing 40,000–50,000 volumes. In April 1891 the library committee recommended the tender received from builders J.&W. Beckett.[48]

The King's Inns archive holds a plan and section by James Franklin Fuller of a proposed book stack for the society (Figs 7.7 and 7.8) which was very much in the Modernist style.[49] It shows a top-lit four-storey circular building of metal construction with a small cupola: nine bookcases on each floor radiate from a

✥ *Fig. 7.9   A crisply carved detail of the chimneypiece, one of two designed by Darley for the reading room.*

Fig. 7.10 *The library showing Fuller's Sullivanesque gable end to the annex.*

central iron spiral staircase. It was to be located to the rear of the building, accessed by a causeway built from the landing outside the door of the library room across the return to a glass-roofed lobby which linked the two buildings. Hidden from view it did not interfere with the streetscape and gave the architect an opportunity to indulge himself in designing an unusually shaped building using glass and iron.

However, in his built annex to the library, Fuller continued the stone exterior, string courses, fenestration, rustication, cornice and balustrade of Darley's building by one bay which he stepped back slightly. The windows on the flank of the building were blocked off except for those at the centre of the first and second floors and gallery level which were formed into doorways to the annex. The chimneypiece, grate and hearth of the reading room were removed and replaced by double doors. Interestingly, this chimneypiece (Fig. 7.9), similar to the remaining one in the room, found its way into what later became the residence of the British ambassador at Glencairn in Dublin.[50] But the interior of this extension is quite different: behind the three-storey façade is a six-storey construction. Like Henri Labrouste's book stack for the Bibliothèque Nationale in Paris (1860–68) which was designed as a top-lit cage with light filtering through iron landings, Fuller built six storeys of bookshelves lit by skylights and windows to the front, side and rear. The five floors were made of 'cast-iron ornamental gratings' and these, together with iron girders and a cast-iron spiral staircase with sixty-four treads and six landings, located to the rear of the building, were supplied by Walter MacFarlane & Co., Glasgow.[51] While Fuller continued Darley's design in the front of his annex, and may have looked to Labrouste for his interior, the gable end of the library is very much in the style of Louis Sullivan (Fig. 7.10). Fuller would have been familiar with Sullivan's skyscrapers in Chicago, where his trademark elongated arcades of fenestration surely inspired the Irish architect.[52] While the society may not have approved of his circular design for the rear of the library, perhaps Fuller could content himself with the Sullivanesque flank to his extension.

[1] Admission of Benchers 1741–92 (KI B1/3–2) f 177.

[2] KI Benchers' Minutes 5 May 1824, p 138; 21 July 1824, p 146.

[3] Littledale, W.F., *The Society of King's Inns, Dublin, Its Origins and Progress* (Dublin 1859) p 27.

[4] 'Old Dublin Mansion-houses: their lordly occupiers in the last century', *The Irish Builder*, 15 June 1893, p 136.

[5] cf. Chapter I, p 6.

[6] Registry of Deeds, Memorial of Indenture, 37 91 21494.

[7] Madden, R.R., *The Literary Life and Correspondence of the Countess of Blessington*, 3 vols (London 1855) Vol. I, p 46.

[8] Gibbs, V., (ed.) *The Complete Peerage* (London 1912); Coleman, J., 'Luke Gardiner (1745–98) An Irish dilettante', *Irish Arts Review Yearbook 1999*, p 161.

[9] Craig, M., p 102.

[10] A.P.W. Malcomson, from his forthcoming book on Nathaniel Clements. My thanks to Dr Malcomson for sending me a draft.

[11] 'Old Dublin Mansion-houses', p 136.

[12] A.P.W. Malcomson, from his forthcoming book on Nathaniel Clements.

[13] According to Malcomson, Boulter's successors took on, voluntarily and as a private transaction, the perpetuity lease of the house; it was not an official residence.

[14] 'Old Dublin Mansion-houses', pp 136–7.

[15] Registry of Deeds, Robinson to Duffy, 5 March 1822, reg. no. 770 7 521942.

[16] 'Old Dublin Mansion-houses', 1 August 1893, pp 177–8. Curiously, Robinson assigned all his interest in the house to William Duffy of Huntstown, a labourer, for ten shillings sterling, in 1823. Duffy then assigned the house to William Finn of Henrietta Street, the society's chief butler, for the sum of forty pounds. Finn held it on behalf of the society and was its caretaker until the commencement of building. Library accounts (KI MS M11/2–1).

[17] Articles of Agreement between King's Inns and Messrs Carolin, builders, 13 October 1825 (KI MS G/6–1).

[18] *Georgian Society Records of Eighteenth Century Domestic Architecture and Decoration in Dublin*, 5 vols (Dublin 1909–13) Vol. II, p 13.

[19] 'Architecture in Ireland', *Dublin University Magazine*, Vol. XXIX (June 1847) pp 707–8.

[20] Craig, M., p 298.

[21] *The Dublin Penny Journal*, Vol. IV, No. 176, 14 November 1835, p 154.

[22] *The Irish Builder and Engineer*, Vol. LVII, No. 19, 11 September 1915, p 397.

[23] *The Dublin Penny Journal*, op. cit., p 153.

[24] Columns to be made of wood. It is not clear which room was called the 'front parlour'. Builders' estimates (KI MS H3).

[25] Formerly the library committee room.

[26] Up to the mid-1980s the kitchen was the office of the under-treasurer.

[27] KI Benchers' Minutes 1819–30, pp 267, 268; KI Benchers' Minutes 1830–35, p 4, pp 11–12.

[28] Standing Committee Minutes 1844–52, June 1851 (KI MS B2/1–1) pp 134–5.

[29] My thanks to Jonathan Armstrong, librarian of the King's Inns, for this information.

[30] Anon., 'Henrietta Street' 19 November 1896, quote from Kenny, C., 'King's Inns and Henrietta Street chambers', *Dublin Historical Record*, Vol. XLVII, No. 2, Autumn 1994, p 165.

[31] KI Benchers' Minutes 1830–35, meeting of Library Committee, 30 May 1832, p 65.

[32] *The Dublin Penny Journal*, op. cit., p 153.

[33] O'Connor was also responsible for the heraldic glass in the chapel of the Royal Hospital, Kilmainham.

[34] KI Library accounts, Henrietta Street, 8 May 1828 (KI MS H3/1–3).

[35] KI Library accounts (KI MS M11/2–1).

[36] KI Benchers' Minutes 1819–30, p 234.

[37] Ibid., p 242.

[38] The only access to the gallery presently is from the spiral staircase in the 1891 annex to the library.

[39] The book room is at the level of the gallery.

[40] KI Benchers' Minutes 1835–44, Library Committee Report, p 159.

[41] The plan refers to document specifications for the repainting and redecoration of the King's Inns and the law library, dated November 1956. KI Committee Book 1889–1920 (B2/1–8).

[42] An entry in the Library Committee Book 1889–1920, dated 7 June 1920, describes the WC at the rear of the ground floor: 'urinal leaking badly and offensive discharge soaking into fabric outside' (KI MS M1/2-4).

[43] KI Benchers' Minutes 1957–64, 26 November 1962.

[44] KI Library accounts, Henrietta Street (KI MS H3/1-3).

[45] KI Benchers' Minutes 1830–35, pp 44–5.

[46] Ibid., p 70.

[47] Standing Committee Meeting, 2 June 1886 (KI MS B2/1–5) p 249.

[48] William Beckett, quantity surveyor in the family business, was the father of writer Samuel Beckett (1906–89).

[49] KI Map drawer M8/1 and M8/4.

[50] David Griffin of the Irish Architectural Archive kindly supplied the information as to the present location of the chimneypiece. Fuller remodelled Glencairn for Boss Croker of Tamany Hall fame in 1904–5 and 1909.

[51] Memorandum of Agreement with Beckett, 4 May 1891 (KI Map drawer M8/6): The cost was £569. Casey, C., *The Building of Ireland: Dublin.* (Yale University Press 2005) p 161.

[52] Sullivan's Auditorium Theatre Building of Roosevelt University, Chicago was built 1886–1889.

'HENRIETTA STREET...
MIGHT BE PURCHASED'

The question of building chambers at Constitution Hill that had occupied the benchers for so long and over which they had constantly procrastinated was gradually abandoned. It was becoming increasingly obvious that Irish barristers preferred the idea of a centralised law library, to which they came from their various residences around the city, to the use of chambers. Tristram Kennedy (1805-1885), however, a member of King's Inns, was convinced of the value of the system of chambers for the training of barristers in Ireland.

Kennedy, who was called to the Bar in 1834, acquired Blessington House, Luke Gardiner's former home in Henrietta Street, in 1837 and converted it into chambers (Fig. 8.1).[1] Two years later he opened his Dublin Law Institute at this address and in 1841 acquired the house next door, number 9.[2] These two were called 'Queen's Inns Chambers Upper' to distinguish them from number 3, the first house in the terrace, which was called 'Queen's Inns Chambers Lower', after it was purchased by Kennedy in 1842.[3] The aim of his institute was to facilitate 'the acquisition of legal knowledge' and to acknowledge 'the great advantage to be derived from a safe and early direction of the studies of those embarking in legal pursuits ...'.[4] However, Kennedy's vision of a coherent system of education for young lawyers eventually collapsed in 1846 due, according to Kenny, to 'professional jealousies' and to the fact that few barristers were willing to take pupils.[5]

But Kennedy was still convinced of the appropriateness of Henrietta Street becoming an enclave for the legal profession and as such an extension of the King's Inns. Many members of the profession lived there from the beginning of the

Fig. 8.1   *Blessingtown House, 10 Henrietta Street, former home of Luke Gardiner, became the Dublin Law Institute in 1839.*

nineteenth century and more came after the library opened in 1832. He published a proposal in 1878 that the society should acquire all of the houses on the street and erect a gateway from Henrietta Lane across to Henrietta Place, thereby creating an annex to the King's Inns.[6] Duhigg had thought along these lines originally. In his *History* (1806) he criticised the benchers for their general mishandling of the site at Constitution Hill, and observed that 'Henrietta Street itself might by this time be purchased, and the present ground form a cheap garden annexed thereto'.[7] At the time of his death in 1885 Kennedy owned the entire terrace from number 3 to number 10 (Blessington House), having owned and sold a number of houses on the opposite side of Henrietta Street.

By the end of the nineteenth century this once elegant and fashionable street, which in its heyday in the mid- to late eighteenth century was home to the cream of Irish society – lords justices, lord chief justices, bishops, peers and prominent MPs, the leaders of the spiritual and temporal life of the capital (and, in the case of the lords primate, combining the two) – was partly in tenements. The movement of the city eastwards had begun much earlier when the earl of Kildare had built Leinster House in a most unfashionable part of the city in 1745. He is said to have remarked at the time 'Wherever I go, fashion will follow me.' Later, John Beresford, by moving the Custom House to the east, ensured that the fashionable did indeed move eastwards. Henrietta Street started its decline, but it was gradual. According to the *Georgian Society Records*, the last peer to live there was Viscount Lorton, second son of the 2nd earl of Kingston, who lived in number 15 until 1828. By 1831 number 11 was occupied by Proctors Thomas Tilly, Joseph Hamilton and Arthur Ormsby, later by N. Kenny, miniature painter and Andrew Castle Montgomery, barrister.[8] The last of the houses to retain some of its former dignity was number 4, which was occupied and maintained by Lady Henrietta (Harriet) Daly, daughter of the earl of Farnham who, after her father's death, continued to live in the house until 1849.[9] But well before that many barristers, solicitors and proctors had come to live on the street, and after the encumbered Estates Court opened its offices in 1851 in number 14, they were joined by civil engineers and surveyors.

In 1892 representatives of Kennedy's estate sold numbers 3–10 to the Rt Hon. Joseph M. Meade, LL.D, Alderman of Dublin, for £4,000. Meade subdivided the grand rooms, removed staircases, sold the chimneypieces to dealers in London, and created 'open-door' tenements, cramming as many families as possible into them. Happily, in 1899 numbers 9 and 10, the 'Queen's Inns Chambers Upper' came into the possession of the Daughters of Charity, who have, at a cost to themselves, maintained these beautiful Pearce houses in good condition and, with number 8, have recently completed a major programme of restoration.

Prior to its purchase by Kennedy in 1837, number 10 (Blessington House) had been briefly considered as a possible acquisition by the King's Inns 'for any purpose to which the Society may think proper to convert it'.[10] However, it was more logical for the King's Inns to expand – if expand they did at all – down the opposite side of the street, where the library stood. Accordingly, the library committee recommended in 1864 the purchase of number 11, the house next door to the library and across the street from number 10, and the society the following year paid the owner, Kennedy, £400 sterling for the property. It was then, apparently, in need of repair. But, unlike most of the houses in the street, including its original mirror image, number 12, it had never been set in tenements.

Compared with the others, number 11 is quite a narrow house, brick built, with four storeys over a basement. The blind windows on three storeys remain a mystery (Fig. 8.2).[11] The strongly defined string and blocking courses give a

Fig. 8.2   Number 11 Henrietta Street.

horizontal emphasis to the façade and originally extended across number 12 also. Windows at ground-floor level have quoined surrounds which, like the string courses, are of Portland stone. The brickwork at third-floor level has been replaced, probably in the twentieth century. The stair hall is wainscoted throughout, the floor is of limestone laid in an unusual pattern, and the main staircase to the right is of Portland stone with wrought-iron balusters. The staircase leads to the first-floor reception rooms only. Of the hall and staircase *The Irish Builder* remarked in 1893:

> Though the entrance hall is not large enough or bold enough, the grade of the stone staircase is admirable: it is easy for the feeblest to ascend. The ironwork connected with the balusters is all hammered metal, and in graceful floriated turns and curves. The walls are done in plaster to represent wainscoting. Over the parlour door is an oval with the three Graces in relief, and on the opposite wall is a corresponding oval or circle with three male figures.[12]

The secondary staircase behind this was altered at the end of the eighteenth century to facilitate access to number 12 at second floor and basement levels. Both staircases are in excellent condition.

To understand this and other alterations and the special relationship between numbers 11 and 12, it is necessary to go back to the eighteenth-century history of both houses.

Luke Gardiner had built numbers 11 and 12 in 1730–33 to designs by Edward Lovett Pearce.[13] The lease of number 11 was bought by the Rt Hon. William Graham, MP for Drogheda, for 999 years from March 1730 at a yearly rent of £16.12s.4d. In February 1735 Henry Boyle, who was Speaker of the House of Commons, 1733–56, and was created earl of Shannon in the latter year, bought the lease for £2,500.[14] His son, Richard, inherited the title and house in 1764 on the death of his father. The previous year he had married the daughter of the Rt Hon. John Ponsonby, Speaker of the House of Commons who, it appears, had come to live in number 6 in 1744. The 2nd earl of Shannon, who lived in number 11 until his death in 1807, extended the accommodation by acquiring the house next door (number 12) in 1780, linking both by doorways broken through the dividing walls.

It is not difficult to see where the doors were cut into the walls to gain access from one house to the other. At ground-floor level there was an opening to the left on entering the house, with another behind the staircase wall, while at first-floor front landing level there is evidence of another opening. On the second floor, flights of stairs are built over existing flights on the secondary staircase, to provide a landing (and an opening) at the level of the new second floor in number 12 which had been raised. The earl was thus presented with a large space for entertaining, as his reception rooms at ground-floor and first-floor levels in number 12 were the full three-bay width of the house.

There have been changes to the hall, not least that of the newer doorway. From the hall a window can be seen on the first landing that gives a view to the hall and stairs. Close to it is a rather puzzling hinged doorway camouflaged in the panelling at first-floor level to the rear of the hall. Probably it facilitated a shortcut from one point to another and was Victorian, as was the convoluted plan of the secondary staircase and walkway at this level. The plasterwork of the ground-floor reception rooms has been executed in different styles (and probably dates) with neo-Classical medallions in the room to the front and a rococo ceiling in the room to the rear. The front parlour now has a mid-nineteenth century floriated centrepiece and a dentilled cornice. Four late eighteenth-century medallions decorate the walls of this room. The nineteenth-century chimneypiece is of Kilkenny marble. Through a wide door is the rear parlour where the ceiling is decorated in the rococo style with small-scale fruit and flowers, stylised shells and flowing acanthus leaves, and a decorated cornice (Fig 8.3). One of the house's two imported Siena marble chimneypieces appears in this room.[15]

The front room at first floor level, Cathal Crimmins believes, was probably panelled in much the same way as the hall. The two windows in the room to the rear which look down into the garden (shortened in 1936 when Dublin Corporation took part of it for a housing scheme) reach as far as the floor. The shutters on these are tripartite. One door from this room leads out to the landing mentioned before, where one can look into the hall from the window. From this point a kitchen is reached across a bridge-type structure[16] (to the rear of the house). The secondary staircase and landings are top-lit and the stairs themselves, curiously, are made of stone (Portland and limestone) from ground- to second-floor level, and of timber at basement and attic levels. The remaining rooms on the next two floors are as one might expect, smaller, with lower ceilings and no decoration.

From 1868 number 11 was the residence of the librarian and under-treasurer of the King's Inns up to 1984 and 1990 respectively, and has over the years been well maintained by the society. In 1887 James Franklin Fuller was asked by the society to look at two proposals for its use: the possibility of providing access from the library into number 11, and the feasibility of converting the house into two apartments. Fuller was of the opinion that both proposals were possible, but would prove to be expensive. A third possibility, he suggested, would be a single tenant and as the house was in good repair it needed only superficial work. This, in his opinion, would be well worth the expense. Happily, none of the proposed works were carried out and the librarian and under-treasurer continued to live in number 11 in their respective apartments.

Fig. 8.3 *Detail of plasterwork on the ceiling of the rear parlour.*

[1] Number 10 Henrietta Street. Previously known as Mountjoy House, this house and number 9 were designed by Edward Lovett Pearce, architect of the Parliament House (now Bank of Ireland).

[2] In 1845 the houses on Henrietta Street were re-numbered due to the addition of another residence on the east side. Number 9 was formerly number 8.

[3] The society did not change its name to 'The Queen's Inns' during the reign of Queen Victoria, as it had during that of Queen Anne.

[4] Kennedy papers, National Library of Ireland, MS 2987.

[5] Kenny, C., *Tristram Kennedy*, p 227.

[6] Kennedy, T., *The State and the Benchers* (Dublin 1878) p 14.

[7] Duhigg, B., p 538.

[8] Proctors were practitioners of law in ecclesiastical and certain other courts, *The New Oxford Dictionary of English* (Oxford 1998); N. Kenny is probably Nicholas Kenny (fl. 1839–56) whose best-remembered work is 'The Irish House of Commons on the 16th April 1782, when Grattan moved the Declaration of Irish Rights' (1844), painted for Henry Grattan jnr. It contains 149 portraits of members and others on the floor of the House and 98 portraits of those in the gallery (Strickland, W.G., *Dictionary of Irish Artists* [Irish University Press 1969] pp 576–8).

[9] *Irish Georgian Society Records*, Vol. II (Dublin 1969) p 19.

[10] KI Benchers' Minutes 1835–44, p 24.

[11] See Casey, C., pp 198–9.

[12] 'Old Dublin Mansion-houses', *The Irish Builder*, 1 August 1893, p 178.

[13] In his 1987 study of numbers 11 and 12 Henrietta Street, architect Cathal Crimmins attributed two drawings by Pearce to number 11 on the basis of notations and dimensions on one of them. These had been attributed previously to number 10. Crimmins, C., 'Henrietta Street: a conservation study', unpublished thesis for M.Arch.Sc. degree in conservation studies (University College Dublin 1987) p 89.

[14] King's Inns, G3/2–2.

[15] An account, addressed to the earl of Shannon and dated 2 December 1788, for '2 ornamental Chimney pieces with Sienna Marble Grounds ...' for £100 including shipping, is among the Shannon Papers in the Public Record Office Northern Ireland D2707/B16. Photostat in Crimmins, C., 1987.

[16] Crimmins calls this a 'Victorian bridge'.

THE BUILDINGS AND
THEIR SURVIVAL

It is tempting to wonder how the King's Inns complex of buildings would have fared had it became the home for the Free State parliament, as *The Irish Builder* proposed in 1924. This proposal had a number of advantages. The site was 'very quickly accessible by tram and is just beside the Broadstone Terminus' and, excepting the library, 'little use is nowadays made of [the King's Inns]'. It suggested further that the library could be left where it is or moved near the law courts, or even to 'the Chapel Royal, Dublin Castle which is not needed as a place of worship there being no longer a Viceregal Establishment'. Houses in Henrietta Street could be used as offices, and the lawns offered 'lots of space for temporary buildings should such be needed'.[1] Happily, for King's Inns, Leinster House was chosen instead.

Another threat to the future of the King's Inns was posed by plans that won first prize in a competition established by the Civics Institute of Ireland in 1914. The aim of the competition was to 'elicit designs and reports of a tentative nature on a plan for "Greater Dublin"', suggesting measures for the development of the city and for its housing needs. If their plans had been adopted the winners, Abercrombie and Kelly, would have erected a cathedral on the site of Henrietta Street and other streets in the vicinity, with the rear of Gandon's building forming part of a piazza behind the church (Fig. 9.1).[2]

By the close of the nineteenth century the King's Inns was in possession of a number of buildings at Constitution Hill and Henrietta Street. James Gandon's building was almost a century old and Frederick Darley's library seventy years old. The dining hall was an historic building and, like the library, the lodges, cottages

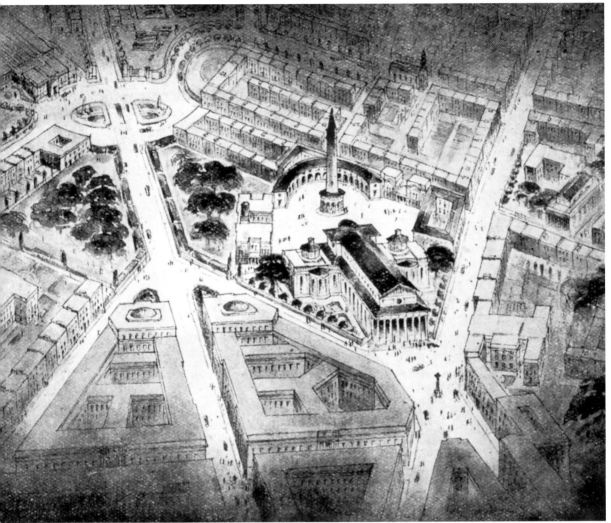

Fig. 9.1   *Abercrombie & Kelly's 'Plan for Dublin of the Future' shows the King's Inns behind the church to the left of the piazza.*

and number 11 Henrietta Street, needed constant attention and repair. Owning buildings of historical importance brings with it a burden of responsibility not just for their immediate maintenance but for their preservation and conservation for generations to come. In economic terms, it has meant that large sums of money have been expended on the upkeep of the society's buildings during the twentieth century and now, at the beginning of a new millennium, that work continues, as will be seen.

The twentieth century saw the undertaking of major renovation projects in order to preserve the fabric of the buildings, in which dampness and dry rot were causing serious and recurring problems. The first programme was initiated in 1930 when the society's architect, John Robinson (from Robinson & Devane, architects), submitted reports to the benchers on the condition of their buildings which showed that repairs were needed across the board.[3] A number of repairs were carried out at this point. What apparently began as a cosmetic exercise in 1956 under William A. Maguire (then architect to the society), when a programme of 'repainting and redecoration' got under way, evolved into a major job in 1959–60 after dry rot was discovered in Gandon's building. The library building in 1961 required repairs to its roof, and to the ceiling of the reading room, and the following year dry rot was discovered in the annex to the library, as has been discussed in Chapter VIII.

By the beginning of the 1980s it was evident that the fabric of the King's Inns needed a great deal of work. This began in 1982 and continued until 1988, in which year a car park was provided in the grounds. During 1998 over a quarter of a million pounds was spent on refurbishment at the main building and the library. The cost to the society of maintaining the cottages was at least £10,000 per annum during the last five years of the century and it was decided in 1999 that a major refurbishment of the cottage block should be undertaken. By September 2000 this had been completed and the cottages were commercially let to tenants. That year too, a major plan was undertaken to enhance the grounds at the King's Inns. This included as its focal point the 'intended line of buildings' for chambers, as drawn on Francis Johnston's plan of 1813, which provides a piazza in front of Gandon's building, in the centre of which 'Henrietta' stands in solitary splendour.[4] These works marked the bicentenary of the laying of the foundation stone of the King's Inns.

GANDON'S BUILDING

Major works were carried out on this building from the 1930s to the end of the century. John Robinson's report of December 1930 lists extensive work that needed to be done but by May 1931 when specifications had been prepared and estimates received, it was clear that only the most urgent jobs could be undertaken at this time. These included the roof over the dining hall, which had been laid to a very flat pitch and needed to be stripped, treated and re-slated with, 'hopefully, old slates'. The chimney stacks were in a dangerous condition and required renewing, as did the ceiling in the pantry. The wine cellars needed ventilation. These were among the works that, in Robinson's opinion, were 'absolutely necessary and urgent'.[5]

One major recommendation not acted upon related to the north wall of the main building on which the plaster was defective and needed to be replaced, a job that was not done until the 1960s under the direction of William Maguire. In his recommendation Robinson gave specific instructions for the 'careful' removal of the existing plasterwork 'saving ornaments, architraves to windows and architrave to main cornice … If it is not possible to save all the enrichments … they should be carefully preserved or replaced with ornaments to exactly correspond to the old' (Fig. 9.2).[6] By the time that Maguire came to repair this part of the building in 1960, the brickwork was saturated and had disintegrated, the plaster was falling off the wall and sections of the stucco roundels (the 'ornaments' mentioned above) had also disintegrated. Maguire removed the mortar plaster, the roundels and the architraves, and renewed the brickwork where necessary. The window heads and reveals were renewed in Portland stone.

In his specification for the painting and decoration of the King's Inns and library in November 1956, Maguire provided for £100 to be set aside 'for coving in the ceiling at both gable ends' of the benchers' room. This was when the *oeil-de-boeuf* windows were removed as 'they served no useful purpose', the amount of light admitted being minimal.[7] Apart from this, the work in the late 1950s was mostly cosmetic, including items such as the cleaning and re-gilding of the chandeliers and mirror in the dining hall. However, in October 1958 dry rot was discovered in the roof over the benchers' room and, having sought a second opinion from Robinson, Keefe & Devane, the society was obliged to reconstruct the roof. This was completed by July 1959. More dry rot was discovered on the north face of the dining hall where the roof trusses had rotted away and the wall was saturated; also in the stairwell where, six weeks after it had been painted, 'mushrooms' appeared on one of the walls. On investigation, it was found that the wall timbers were like powder. The gutters were renewed and steel joists were placed in the walls.

Early in 1981 it was agreed that repairs were urgently needed to the fabric of the King's Inns. The estimate 'for masonry and boundary wall work' was somewhat in excess of £500,000. The work progressed slowly and it was not until April 1988 that the restoration of the exterior was completed.[8] Work then commenced on extensive refurbishment of the interior of the King's Inns. This included painting and decoration as well as new concrete floors in the basement, re-sanding the dining-hall floor, restoration of the oval ceiling light in the stairwell and the provision of two brass handrails on the staircase to the dining hall. During 1987 glazed entrance porches had been provided at the main entrance to the building and at the entrance from the courtyard to prevent drafts, but happily these were removed in the 1990s. Also removed in 1998 were eight layers of paint from the eight granite pilasters in the entrance hall. That year too saw a number of projects being undertaken including the refurbishment of the kitchen, new toilet facilities off the dining hall, and the conversion of the old laundry room into a tutorial room. The society's annual report for 1999 proudly announced the restoration of another Gandon interior. The small office to the south of the staircase in the entrance hall (formerly the office of the under-treasurer), where the ceiling had been lowered by six feet and the window onto the courtyard divided, had its partitions removed.

LIBRARY

General maintenance continued on the library building in Henrietta Street throughout the twentieth century and included William Maguire's 1956 programme of re-painting and redecoration. They seem to have been badly needed at this stage. An article on the King's Inns in *The Irish Tatler and Sketch* of October 1958 drew attention to the contrast between 'the gloomy, decaying atmosphere of the Library and the beauty and sparkling brightness of the newly decorated Dining Hall and Benchers' Rooms in the North Wing'. The splendour of the building, the writer asserted, was 'obliterated by dark paint and mouldering walls and ceilings'.[9]

In his 1960 report on the condition of the library Maguire recommended a number of works to be carried out which included roof repairs. It was found that a deflection of the tie beam that carried the ceiling of the reading room was causing that ceiling to sag resulting in the plaster cracking. Two years later the benchers agreed to accept a quotation for roof and ceiling repairs to the reading room at £5,208.[10] While the work on the ceiling proceeded, the marvellous centrepiece remained *in situ* and the loose plaster was cut away and replaced.[11] Many of the outer panels of the stained-glass window in the landing were replaced with selected hand-made antique glass by the State Glass Co. Ltd.[12]

In 1997, during a refurbishment programme, some interesting wallpapers were found in the offices of the under-treasurer and of the dean. The former room contains large areas of a floral paper with flock border that dates to 1850–60. A portion of it is preserved *in situ*, behind the glazed bookcases. The other wallpapers were in the dean's office, where a *faux bois* scheme imitating wood panelling was discovered. It was thought at first that this was the original wallcovering of 1830, but this dating had to be revised to closer to the middle of the century when an earlier wallpaper and border were found beneath, pasted directly onto the unpainted plaster surface. The wallpaper conservator, David Skinner, found part of a name stamped on the lining paper and concluded that the supplier of the paper was Patrick Boylan, who was trading as a 'house painter, decorator, gilder, manufacturer of stained paper and floor cloth' at 102 Grafton Street and 49 Lower Baggot Street. The pattern consists of a vertical arrangement of Pompeiian motifs linked by trailing ivy. It is presumed to be French and it is likely to have been manufactured in France in the mid-1820s (Fig. 9.3).[13]

The *faux bois* paper (Figs. 9.4 and 9.5) imitates oak and after the lengths were hung they were embellished with borders and decorative pieces such as cut-out 'capitals' and 'bases' applied to narrow bands or borders, simulating pilasters. This scheme of wallpaper survived completely throughout the room, only hidden in places by white emulsion paint after the bookcases had been installed. The paint has been removed successfully and damaged areas restored. Interestingly, the skirting is painted in *faux*-mahogany, and two areas, one a section of window architrave close to the fireplace, and the other the door facing the under-treasurer's office (both of which had been hidden by bookcases) show original honey-coloured *faux*-oak graining. As was noted in the annual report of 1997, 'the preservation of the room is deemed to be an important contribution to the national heritage'.[14]

11 HENRIETTA STREET

The house at 11 Henrietta Street was well maintained by the society throughout the century with general repairs made in the 1930s under John Robinson and more extensive work carried out in the 1960s under William Maguire. This latter work included the removal of the parapet and coping and of the brick facing to floor level on the top storey, as the bricks had become porous and were disintegrating. The rest of the façade was re-pointed at the same time. In 1989 £8,000 was spent on redecorating and repairs to the house.[15] As neither the under-treasurer nor the librarian continued to reside in the property on a permanent basis, the society found that it had no real use for it and rented it for a couple of years in the mid-1990s to the Registry of Deeds (which was being refurbished) and then to an interdenominational school between 2000 and 2002. Following receipt of a survey that had been carried out under the auspices of the City Council, the society realised that serious repairs and conservation were required. The zoning for the area meant that the use had to be 100 per cent residential or at least 50/50 office/residential. By 2005 planning permission had been granted for use of the four main floors for educational purposes, with a residential apartment in the spacious basement. During most of 2005 and 2006 a team of leading conservators and builders under the direction of the society's architect, Cathal Crimmins, worked with the objective of bringing the property into full use. The result is heartening: the main rooms of the house are in constant use by the students of the King's Inns; and the delicate plasterwork in the entrance hall and rear rooms on ground and first floors has been revealed after layers of paint were removed. The windows have been repaired and the fine Portland stone of their surrounds has been restored. In addition, the cement pointing has been removed and replaced with lime tuck-pointing. The structural problems in the basement were resolved, albeit at great expense. The benchers must take credit for having undertaken such a painstaking and forbidding project. It is also heartening to find so much activity on Henrietta Street once more.

COTTAGES AND LODGES

In his report on the society's buildings in 1930, John Robinson outlined in some detail the condition of the cottages and lodges (which together numbered nine at that time), the accommodation provided in each, and particulars of the tenants.[16] The problems were common to all of the houses – ceilings unsafe, dampness, many floors had rotted, roofs needed repair, and all stonework was in bad condition. None had gas, electricity, or bathroom facilities. Four of the cottages in the block had water closets in the yard, all but one needing replacement, and all five houses took their water from one tap in the yard.[17] The north lodge on Constitution Hill, and the cottage on the boundary wall with number 10 Henrietta Street were in bad repair and were demolished on Maguire's recommendations in 1953 and 1964 respectively.[18] The remaining dwellings comprise: five making up the L-shaped block of cottages to the south of the Registry of Deeds, the south lodge on Constitution Hill (all to designs by Jacob Owen) and the other to the rear of the dining hall, behind Francis Johnston's archway and designed by him (Fig. 9.6). The south gate lodge was refurbished in summer 2004 and is now occupied by tenants.

The cottages were occupied up to the late 1990s. In 1999 plans were drawn up to renovate the block of five cottages and by September 2000 the society had tenants, each on one-year leases, living in them. The society and its architect, Cathal Crimmins, have taken much care to conserve the integrity of these sturdy blackstone dwellings while providing modern facilities within them. Access to the

Fig. 9.6 *Part of the L-shaped block of five cottages built by Jacob Owen in 1837.*

cottages for residents and their guests is through the gate next to the library in Henrietta Street. The cost of the renovation was IR£350,000 which was financed by means of a bank loan. The operation has been 'ring fenced' and it is expected to have the loan paid off by 2015.

KING'S INNS PARK AND GROUNDS

As we saw, in 1836 Jacob Owen levelled the uneven terrain to the north and north-west of the gardens. Along the inns' northern boundary, the Rope Walk, where the River Bradoge used to flow, the society's neighbour Lord Palmerston (who happened to be prime minister at the time) came to an agreement with King's Inns in 1861 that the Walk should be removed and that a boundary wall would be built by him along the site.[19] Some years later in 1878, the Dublin Artisans Dwellings Company built Temple Cottages close to the new wall and then, 'being in want of a way, or passage in front of said cottages', applied to the society for a strip of their land measuring ten feet wide along that boundary. Permission was granted.

Fig. 9.7   The tree trunk that has become attached to one of the seats in the park.

It is not known when the very attractive wrought-iron garden seats appeared in the grounds of the King's Inns or who made them. William Maguire remembers two being there in the 1950s, one of which is the famous seat to which long ago the tree trunk attached itself at the south end of the grounds (Fig. 9.7). In 1987 he had ten copies cast and all eleven can be seen in the park.[20] In 1988 the Office of Public Works refurbished the gates at the top of Henrietta Street at a cost in excess of £25,000,[21] and four years later, in 1992, the society refurbished the wrought-iron railings and gates on Constitution Hill.[22] The cost of this was £89,807.[23] The landscaping of the car park, which was completed in November 1988, has worked well for the society, quietly tucked away as it is to one side of Gandon's building.[24]

To celebrate the bicentenary of the laying of the foundation stone of the King's Inns in 2000, a plan aimed at enhancing the grounds was carried out by Crimmins and landscape architect Gerry Mitchell. The tarmac in the courtyard between the dining hall and the Registry of Deeds was removed and cobbles were laid between the two granite-paved footpaths and granite flags were placed under Johnston's arch. A curved retaining wall of granite in front of the King's Inns gives life to Francis Johnston's 1813 drawing of the 'intended line of buildings' for chambers, providing a piazza which successfully sets off this historic building.

The King's Inns complex of buildings is a uniquely important group of eighteenth- and nineteenth-century buildings, designed in whole or in part by a number of Ireland's greatest architects, Edward Lovett Pearce, James Gandon, Francis Johnston, and also Frederick Darley and James Franklin Fuller. The burden of caring for this sizeable portion of Ireland's architectural heritage is not to be underestimated. These are not museum pieces but house a living, working institution. The training of barristers continues; the dining hall hosts commons during term time and various other functions during the rest of the year. The library is well used by students and lawyers alike. The recent work on number 11 Henrietta Street demonstrates the commitment that the King's Inns has to its properties and to its determination to ensure that their doors will continue to be open to future generations of students, barristers, the local community and to the public at large. Despite the false starts in the building history of the King's Inns, the society finally found its home where, over the past two hundred years, it has managed to maintain its buildings in good condition and is committed, by all appearances, to looking after them for future generations.

1 *Irish Builder*, Vol. LXVI, 19 April 1924, p 317.

2 Abercrombie, P., Kelly, A., and Kelly, S., *Dublin of the Future: the new town plan* (Liverpool and London 1922).

3 King's Inns MS H2/3 1930–33.

4 According to C.S. Curran, this statue was originally in the rotunda of the Four Courts where it remained up to 1880, after which it disappeared, only to reappear in the grounds of King's Inns.

5 Robinson to J. Carton, under-treasurer, 1 May 1931 (KI MS H2/3).

6 Report on Main Buildings, King's Inns, 5 December 1930. John J. Robinson to J. Carton, under-treasurer and librarian (KI MS H2/3).

7 Conversation with William Maguire, July 2000.

8 KI Annual Report 1988.

9 O'Neill, M., 'The King's Inns' in *The Irish Tatler and Sketch*, October 1958, pp 18–20.

10 KI Benchers' Minutes 1957–64, 11 April 1962.

11 Conversation with William Maguire, 20 February 2001.

12 KI Benchers' Minutes 1957–64, November/December 1962.

13 Report on wallpaper conservation in the Library Building of the King's Inns, Henrietta Street, David Skinner, King's Inns, October 1997.

14 KI Annual Report 1997.

15 KI Annual Report 1989.

16 Report on cottages by John Robinson, 21 November 1930. King's Inns archives H2/3/1930–33.

17 The servants of the society had requested electric light at the cottages in 1934, but this was refused due to lack of funds. However, at a benchers' meeting on 11 October 1943 it was decided to supply the cottages with electricity, but the question of a direct water supply to them was postponed.

18 Standing Committee Minutes 1960–75, 15 December 1964.

19 Standing Committee Minutes, B2/1–3 1846–73, 21 October 1861. A boundary wall can be seen on the Ordnance Survey map of 1838, revised 1864.

20 No trace has been found of the second original seat mentioned by Maguire.

21 Standing Committee Minutes, 26 April 1988.

22 Conversation with William Maguire, July 2000.

23 Council Minutes, 14 May 1992. Council Minute Book 1979–1992.

24 The total cost of the work was £153,792. KI Annual Report 1988.

INDEX